Deadline

A play

Geoff Bateman
and
Emlyn Pritchard

Samuel French – London
New York – Sydney – Toronto – Hollywood

FOR AMATEUR PRODUCTION ENQUIRIES

UNITED KINGDOM AND WORLD
EXCLUDING NORTH AMERICA

plays@samuelfrench.co.uk

020 7255 4302/01

Each title is subject to availability from Samuel French, depending upon country of performance.

CHARACTERS

Cathy Vanagio
Tony Westerby
Alex Conrad
Dinah Conrad
Taxi Driver (voice off)
Detective Inspector Weaver
Badger

The action takes place in the lounge of Alex Conrad's converted farmhouse on the south coast.

Time—the present

PRODUCTION NOTES

In Act I, Scene 3, it is important that when Cathy brings out the already-bloodied bedsheet with which to cover Tony's "dead" body she displays/drapes it in such a way that the audience can see it is already bloody while Dinah cannot. (See p. 31)

It is suggested that the smaller cupboard door has a latch that can be operated from the inside as well as from the front, so that in Act II, Scene 1, Cathy can work the door from inside, pushing it open on cue. (See p. 50)

In Act II, Scene 3, Alex must drop the paper-knife behind the sofa, to be able to reach it later unnoticed. (See pp. 63 and 67)

ACT 1

SCENE 1

The lounge of Alex Conrad's converted farmhouse. A Friday afternoon in October. The room reflects an atmosphere of pleasant comfort and the orderly manner of the owner. French windows in the back wall L open out onto a paved patio beyond which grassland stretches to a clifftop overlooking the sea

A staircase comes down and around the side of the room R beneath which are two storage cupboards, one smaller than the other as the angle of the staircase recedes; the sides of the staircase are oak panelled and help to camouflage the cupboards. An arched entrance UR provides access from the kitchen and the main door of the house. UL is a door leading to a spare room

Between the entrance and the french windows are bookshelves housing a large collection of detective novels, several of which are first editions. The continuity of the bookshelves is broken by an alcove with a buffet upon which are drinks decanters, glasses etc. Above the alcove hangs an abstract painting. Patterned curtains hang at the french windows and a period carpet covers most of the floor

DR is a desk with a swivel chair. On the desk is a lamp and telephone and above the desk hangs an abstract painting by Cathy Vanagio. DL is a combination unit which stores high-fidelity equipment and a collection of records and tapes. Above the unit hangs another abstract painting by Cathy Vanagio; it is unfortunate that the paintings seem to detract from the room's symmetry

A standard lamp occupies the corner of the room UL and DL is an armchair. At an angle left of centre of the room is a sofa in front of which a coffee table completes the room's furnishings

As the curtain rises, Cathy Vanagio is seated at the desk, writing perhaps a letter. She is an attractive American, twenty-two or twenty-three years old. She has short hair and is wearing a light-coloured blouse over denim jeans that reveal splodges of paint. The curtains at the french windows are open to reveal the late afternoon of the dull October day

Tony Westerby appears outside the french windows. He is in his mid-thirties, obviously a well-cared-for person, and is wearing a thick sweater and dark trousers. He looks into the room, sees Cathy at the desk and observes her for a moment. Slowly and quietly, he opens the french doors; as he does so, the sound of waves crashing against the cliffs beyond can be heard faintly but clearly—it is this sound that causes Cathy to raise her head momentarily, then she resumes writing. Tony, an air of menace about him, creeps stealthily into the room and moves past the sofa towards Cathy, who now sensing someone in the room, turns and sees Tony's menacing profile. Panicking, Cathy quickly opens the top right-hand drawer of the desk and fumbles for something inside. Tony tries to grab her but she is able to push him away and he stumbles back against the sofa. Cathy reaches into the drawer again, pulls out a revolver and, as Tony makes another lunge at her, she shoots him. He staggers backwards against the sofa, his face locked in a contorted gaze of surprise and death, and as he falls to the floor, apparently dead, his arm dislodges a cushion on the side of the sofa. Cathy drops the revolver and stares at the body in disbelief

Alex Conrad enters from the spare room. He is in his late forties, impressive, and dressed in a sports jacket and slacks. He is wearing his club tie, and in his breast pocket a plain silk handkerchief can be seen clearly. He does not seem too concerned over the scene before him

Alex Is he dead?
Cathy (*moving nearer Tony's body*) I guess so.
Alex Have we overlooked anything? (*He closes the french windows*)
Cathy I guess not.

Cathy picks up the revolver and, as she does so, Tony, as if in a last despairing act, grabs at her, startling her

Alex (*turning*) What about one more rehearsal? That last attempt was somewhat untidy. (*He moves to side of the sofa near Cathy*)
Tony (*rising, smoothing out his trousers*) Untidy? (*Suavely*) I thought my performance was rather impressive. It was Mary Poppins here who nearly screwed it up. (*He moves CL*) Anyway, you might as well forget the whole idea—she won't fall for it.
Alex (*picking up the cushion and plumping it*) If you'll put a little less life into being dead, Dinah will be convinced she's killed you.
Tony I don't really believe this—you're determined to go ahead, aren't you?
Alex I've arranged everything for tonight. (*He stops plumping the cushion*) I do hope you're not about to express reservations.
Tony Express reservations? Everything depends on a bizarre sequence of co-incidences, and if we bungle any part of this absurd caper—
Cathy (*slouching on to the chair*) Ter-rific!
Alex (*moving towards Tony*) Tony, look, we planned this conspiracy together and agreed all the odds are stacked in our favour, so what can possibly go wrong?
Tony Dinah might fumble for the gun like Cathy did, and the longer I have to stand about waiting for her to shoot me, the more chance she has of recognizing me.
Cathy I thought you said she'd never met you?
Tony She might *realize* who I am, or she might have seen my picture in *New Scientist*.

Alex (*placing the cushion back on the sofa*) When was *your* picture in *New Scientist*?

Tony The trade convention—don't you remember?

Alex (*thinking*) I vaguely recall something about that, but it was over a year ago. Anyway, Dinah doesn't subscribe to *New Scientist*, *House and Garden* more like, so there isn't the slightest chance of her recognizing you.

Cathy Maybe Tony should wear a mask.

Alex What the hell for? He's ugly enough as it is. (*To Tony*) Anything else bothering you?

Tony Dinah might figure out it's a set up and call our bluff. If she does, we'll look like a vaudeville act.

Alex She won't call our bluff—the last thing the darling of Fleet Street will want to become involved in is a murder scandal. (*He picks up the newspaper from the coffee table*) Imagine the front page headline ... "Dinah Conrad in Murder Drama"—"I thought he was a prowler says Agony Aunt". Hardly the type of publicity she needs to preserve her prestigious career. (*He tosses the newspaper on to the sofa left*) Oh no, Dinah wouldn't dare call our bluff. I promise you she'll concede defeat willingly—though I doubt graciously.

Tony You seem to forget that your reputation precedes you. You manipulate people with the sly cunning of a fox, and Dinah surely knows that.

Alex That's an appalling slur—

Tony You use people as pawns, gambling with their money, their assets, for your own selfish gains. You destroy any feelings of respect, loyalty and trust, so how can you be sure she'll react as you anticipate?

Alex (*picking up his glass from the coffee table and heading for the buffet*) Because I was married to Lady Macbeth for ten turbulent years, during which time I discovered most of her passions, fears and aversions. Tonight we re-create her most unrelenting fear—a fear of being trapped in a corner, an assailant in pursuit. It's a phobia, a recurring nightmare she's had from childhood—you know the type—you're trying to escape from someone but don't seem able to run quickly enough—your feet are like lead weights. (*He mixes something on the rocks, and laughs to himself*) I remember one occasion, when she lived here at the cottage—I was away on business at the time—she went out to close the barn doors which had blown open with the wind. (*He moves towards Tony*) When she returned, she heard voices from the kitchen, thought burglars were ransacking the place, so she dashed over to the Iredale's farm and had them call the police. Know what they found when they got here? She'd left the radio on! (*He takes a swig of his drink*) "Yesterday in Parliament", I think it was.

Tony An interesting reminiscence, but I seem to have missed the point.

Alex The point is, you have nothing to fear. She'll shoot you first and ask questions later. Drink?

Tony (*declining the offer*) Most reassuring, but I won't go through with all this slapstick clowning. We simply won't pull it off.

Cathy (*rising angrily, waving the revolver*) Now just a minute, I'm giving up my whole weekend to be part of this charade.

Tony Yes, but you're not doing it for love, you're doing it for five grand.

Cathy Five grand? (*She turns on Alex*) You agreed ten!

Alex (*uneasily*) With—Tony's approval.

Tony (*moving towards Alex*) Let's get this straight—you're telling me we're to pay her five thousand *each*?

Alex I assumed you wouldn't object. (*He takes another swig of his drink*)

Tony My share is secured—Cathy is *your* liability, old boy.

Cathy (*waving the revolver again*) I agreed to act as your witness for ten grand and that's the least I need to get my studio off the ground. (*She stops waving the revolver about as if only just realizing she is still holding it, and puts it on top of the desk*)

Tony (*to Alex*) You should have consulted with me before making a deal like that.

Alex Give the girl a break, what's five thousand when you're about to make a million? Cathy is an integral part of the plot.

Tony Plot? (*He starts to pace towards the hi-fi then turns*) You read too many detective stories, old boy. I keep trying to tell you this isn't a whodunnit where all the pieces of the jigsaw fit neatly into place and the villain is caught. Your *plot* has too many loopholes.

Cathy (*moving towards the main entrance*) This is just fantastic. Do you know, just for a moment I was getting kind of excited about all this. If you *do* ever reach a decision, let me know. *I'm* going to finish that painting for Colonel Foxcroft.

Alex moves towards Cathy to try and placate her but she ignores him and is about to storm out of the room when she turns, angry

This would really have been some big deal for me.

Cathy exits

Alex (*turning to Tony*) Great, now you've upset Cathy. (*He takes a large swig of his drink*)

Tony I'm real sore about that. Goody-two-shoes comes out of this rather well for an evening's work, doesn't she? I get my head blown off and she makes ten grand.

Alex I don't understand why you're so uptight about everything—after all, it was *your* idea.

Tony Not exactly my idea—the inspiration came from a thriller you loaned to me.

Alex Ah yes, you mean *Calibre*? (*He goes to the bookshelves and puts his glass on the buffet*)

Tony (*casually*) Is that what it's called?

Alex (*picking out the first book on the shelf*) *Calibre*, by Edward Chesney Abcot, a clever but little-known mystery thriller. Did you know this is a first edition? Who ever would have thought this ailing manuscript would provide the key to my fortune? If everything comes off, remind me to send a donation to the Thriller Writer's Benevolent Fund. (*He thumbs through the book*)

Tony If everything comes off? You hint at uncertainty. If by chance, Dinah's read it, you can of course kiss the idea goodbye.

Alex She isn't into thrillers and anyway, this hasn't been re-printed for years and there are very few copies now in circulation. I found this at a dealer on the Charing Cross Road and none of the libraries I checked out had a copy. (*Scanning the pages*) Eleanor, the unsuspecting heroine of the novel, will tonight be played by my beloved Dinah, except that our ending is slightly different, and, may I modestly suggest, more ingenious. We rig a fake murder to *avoid* paying the blackmailer. (*He replaces the book on the shelf*)

Tony You can hardly describe Dinah as a blackmailer.

Alex (*topping up his drink*) She will otherwise receive substantial sums to which she is not really entitled.

Tony She is under the terms of your divorce settlement, old boy.

Alex So we undertake an exercise in skulduggery to adjust the balance of power. Are you sure you won't have a drink?

Tony If it's on the house, I'll have a large brandy.

Alex (*surprised*) Brandy? I thought you were a ginger-ale freak.

Tony All this cloak and dagger stuff has left me with an extremely large knot in my stomach.

Alex pours Tony's drink and collects his own

If you hadn't settled with Dinah out of court, you wouldn't have got into this mess.

Alex (*going towards Tony and handing him his drink*) I had no alternative. Had we gone to court, Dinah might have successfully claimed the cottage, and since this land has belonged to generations of Conrads, I don't see what right she had to it. (*He raises his glass*) Cheers, to lost battles and recovered fortunes. (*He takes a large swig of his drink*)

Tony Lost battles are one of the inequitable hazards of divorce, old boy, so, out of court, you very foolishly agreed to pay her one half of your income for how long was it? Five years?

Alex Unless she re-marries earlier.

Tony And what are the chances of that? (*He sips his brandy*)

Alex Diminishing rapidly, I should think. Who'd want to marry an old dragon like her—exhaling fire in every sentence she writes. Actually, I suspect she's having some kind of affair, but I haven't been able to prove anything, and I doubt if it will flourish.

Tony Especially since she's now a highly successful Fleet Street journalist, a career woman who won't want to be tied down with family responsibilities again.

Alex Don't tell me you've been reading her column.

Tony No, just stating a fact, so you're stuck with the arrangement unless you get out of it tonight—assuming I agree to your plan. Wouldn't you feel guilty over tricking her out of her money?

Alex (*considering his drink*) I invested a large amount of my capital in your project, so I don't regard *her* as being entitled to half *my* share of the profits. I doubt I'd feel guilty over denying her what is legally hers, since, as you so astutely point out, she is one of the most popular writers on Fleet Street, and her own income is more than sufficient to keep her in unashamed luxury until that great features editor up there sends for her final column, and what a relief that will be for everyone. (*He takes another swig of his drink*)

Tony The honourable way would be to try and re-negotiate the settlement with her, she might play ball.

Alex (*with a hesitant laugh*) She never plays ball. She'd know I had an interesting deal on the cards and drive her usual hard bargain. She wouldn't write the most widely-read column on the Street if she wasn't a determined woman, and there's only one way I can extract her claws from me for good. (*He puts his drink on the coffee table, picks up the newspaper and opens it out*) "Dear Dinah—Your Problem Answered". (*He shows the page to Tony*) Observe how she starts nearly every reply with "I know exactly how you feel". It's her personal jibe at me, of course, causes me considerable distress by implying that she experienced all her readers' problems with me. Her invidious advice makes me feel such a sham. (*He tosses the newspaper on to the sofa*) What angers me even more is that I don't seem to have a right of reply. Unless I can put a stop to the whole distasteful exposé now, it's likely to outrun *The Archers*. (*He pauses*) Tonight is absolutely the last chance I have of luring Dinah here to the cottage, so you're not going to back down, are you? You will help me out of one hell of a mess by playing the fearsome intruder?

Tony (*pacing about*) I've told you, the whole plan is too ridiculous and can't possibly work. I'm sorry I even suggested it—it was meant as a wisecrack and I never intended you to seriously consider—

Alex (*chasing Tony*) Of course it will work. The idea is perfect *and* totally foolproof. Look what we have—a fake murder. Dinah doesn't know that—to her it's all real and she'll think only of her own position and plead for total discretion. Nothing's reported to the police because there isn't anything to report. She'll be convinced I've disposed of your body and she'll never realize the trap she fell into because she's no idea what you look like—and won't have because the room will be dark. In fact, you were so confident there wasn't a chance of her ever recognizing you at some time in the future that you didn't even want me to give a false name to Dinah. You were quite insistent that that wouldn't be necessary.

Tony (*considering his drink*) If I won't do it?

Alex We have to wait two more years before we can register your patent, and someone else might get in ahead of us—like the last time. (*He finishes his drink in one determined gulp*)

Tony I'm not prepared to wait that long or take that risk.

Alex Quite understandable, and it wasn't my fault someone else was working on the same idea—last time. You did all that research for nothing and I must recoup the money I lost. This time I feel confident we're going to hit the jackpot. (*He puts his glass on the coffee table*)

Tony (*pacing the room*) It seems I have no alternative. If I agree, you'll register the patent?

Alex That's the whole idea isn't it? We register the patent, your discovery will astound the world's greatest minds and who knows, a Nobel prize?

Tony (*with a sarcastic laugh*) Have you found anyone interested in the production rights?

Alex I have a company in mind, and don't overlook the royalties from licencing and the worldwide patents. I estimate we'll gross over a million in the first year. (*He rubs his hands together with glee*) And Dinah's not going to get a single, solitary penny!

Tony Which company do you have in mind?

Alex I haven't been able to approach them yet because you only let me have the remaining specifications yesterday. I'll let you know after I've spoken with them because we don't want another mix-up, do we?

Tony I don't know why you have to be so damned secretive. We are supposed to be partners.

Alex I don't want to risk another leaking of information—you know, a wrong word here, a slip of the tongue there. I don't want there to be the slightest chance of a lost fortune this time round.

Tony Speaking of lost fortunes, are you serious about investing in the Vanagio studio? (*He finishes his drink and puts the glass on the coffee table*)

Alex I promised Cathy I'd help her career, and I'm not one to go back on my word.

Tony I don't wish to seem unkind, but her paintings are a disaster. (*He goes toward the desk and points to the painting above it*) I still say that one is hung upside down.

Alex (*also going toward the desk*) It's hung correctly.

Tony (*appraising the painting*) How can you be certain?

Alex Because Cathy always signs her name in the bottom corner.

Tony Maybe Cathy doesn't know which way up it's supposed to be.

Alex If you understood anything at all about art, you'd know that in ugliness there is beauty.

Tony (*moving C*) Since when were you an art critic? I think you just keep buying Cathy's paintings so she'll tag on to you—a boost to your flagging ego—a contest of one-up-manship to try and convince Dinah you're not quite yet ready for the breaker's yard.

Alex (*also moving C*) Not so. I scent a profitable return once Cathy has established herself, so take my advice and buy a couple of her paintings now, while they're still relatively inexpensive.

Tony (*now studying the painting above the hi-fi*) I admire your flair for business, but not your taste in art. I prefer something I can recognize, like the seascape in the hall. That IS a picture.

Alex Dinah chose that but I find it sleazy and commercial, and it's available from any branch of Boots.

Tony (*moving back to C*) One can almost hear the sea crashing against the rocks, feel the rain lashing into one's face—which reminds me, I think we're in for a storm tonight.

Alex Are we?

Tony (*picking up the newspaper*) According to this morning's forecast. (*He searches through the pages for the forecast*)

Alex Hmm, I hope that doesn't deter Dinah from coming, she's terrified of thunder—usually hides under the bed 'till it's over.

Tony (*reading from the forecast*) Here we are—"thunderstorms will develop later in the evening". (*He closes the newspaper and places it on the coffee table*) I hope I don't get soaked waiting for your signal—there isn't any cover out there.

Alex Borrow Cathy's umbrella.

Tony (*heading for the buffet with his glass*) I'll probably die of pneumonia while you're trying to convince Dinah that she's fatally wounded me. (*He mixes another drink*)

Alex Do help yourself to my wine cellar.

Tony If she'd re-married, there'd be no need for all the theatrics.

Alex Theatrics?

Tony (*turning*) You do have all the moves plotted like a stage thriller. (*He moves towards Alex*)

Alex (*starting to pace the room*) I hadn't thought of it quite like that. (*He stops*) Yes, I see what you mean. All the action takes place in one room?

Tony (*after a big swig of his drink*) Correct.

Alex (*pacing again, then hesitating*) But only four characters—the classic stage thriller always has five.

Tony The prowler—he's your fifth character. You did make that report to the police?

Alex Yes, should Dinah decide to check the prowler story with them, they'll confirm it. (*Pacing again*) It *does* have all the essential ingredients of a thriller, doesn't it?

Tony (*with a slight nod*) A darkened room—

Alex A mysterious intruder—

Tony A gunshot—

Alex A blank bullet. In fact, all it lacks is a surprise ending.

Tony You mean I survive?

Alex (*a little puzzled*) Of course you do . . . why shouldn't you?

Tony Nothing—just a thought. (*He takes a swig of his drink*)

Alex (*approaching Tony*) Just a thought about what?

Tony (*moving away*) Oh, call it plot development.

Alex (*stopping*) What exactly do you mean, plot development? We've covered all the angles.

Tony Not *all* the angles—I figured out a surprise ending.

Alex What are you talking about? Why do we need a surprise ending?

Tony (*after a moment's thought*) Doesn't the idea of real murder appeal to you?

Alex *Real* murder? What are you suggesting? (*He pauses for thought*) Oh no, Jesus, you can't be serious. Bump Dinah off? . . . Her readers would never forgive us!

Tony (*moving nearer the bookshelves*) It wasn't Dinah I had in mind. (*He puts his glass on the buffet*)

Alex Not . . . Dinah? But—who else is there?

Tony Alex, you surprise me. (*Running a finger along a row of books*) Chandler, Cheyney (*moving along, reading the authors*) Gardner, not to mention the late Edward Chesney Abcot, to whom you may shortly be indebted. What I mean, Alex Conrad, connoisseur of the murder mystery, honorary member of the "Thriller of the Month Club", is that you have here a wealth of plots, unexpected developments and startling twists. With such an elaborate law library at your disposal, with the jaws of temptation wide open for you, it would be more than naïve of me not to suspect that you intend to do me in.

Alex (*feigning incredulity*) *Do you in?* What on earth for?

Tony You want motives, I'll give you a typewritten list.

Alex Tony, I think you'd better clarify.

Tony (*after a slight pause*) Okay, here's my synopsis. (*Moving nearer Alex*) You switch the blank bullets and have Dinah shoot me—no change to the plan except it's for real. Dinah pleads with you to cover up for her, to protect her fame, and you register *our* patent in your own name and become enormously rich.

Alex Brilliant.

Tony Of course, you'd have to pay Cathy off, unless——

Alex (*a little angrily*) Unless what?

Tony Unless you eliminated her as well.

Alex This is all most fascinating.

Tony And you never thought of it?

Alex (*almost triumphantly*) Of course I thought of it, but there is one small weakness to your plot—there *isn't* a surprise ending. What you suggest is the obvious thing for me to do, so where is the unexpected development, the startling twist?

Tony The surprise is—there isn't one!

Alex Now there's a real shocker, guaranteed to have an audience demanding refunds. No surprise ending? I can't buy that, why—it's almost as criminal as introducing the murderer in the final page—doesn't give the reader a chance to figure it out. I admit that the idea briefly crossed my mind—solely out of a morbid curiosity of course, but I could never bring myself to perpetrate actual murder. You have my word that when the clock strikes twelve, you will walk out into the night, and come morning, Dinah will be quite convinced that I've disposed of your body.

Tony You try to sound *so* reassuring, but don't forget I'm the one who has to look down the gun barrel.

Alex (*placing an arm around Tony's shoulder*) Tone, how long have we known each other?

Tony (*somewhat wary*) A year?

Alex Two years and five months, to be exact, and during that time haven't I given you my full and complete support?

Tony (*moving away*) I suppose so.

Alex Didn't I give my full backing to your last idea when we were so unfortunately beaten with the patent?

Tony nods in agreement

Haven't I financed all your research and equipment, without question? Financial support your family has always refused to give you. Didn't I rescue you from the depths of despair?

Tony You've been like a father to me.

Alex Don't patronize.

Tony Surely you can understand why I can't help but feel I could be the first prize in a game of Russian roulette?

Alex You're still not entirely happy about this, are you?

Tony Does it show?

Alex You could take out extra health insurance.

Tony gives a short laugh

Look, you're my partner and you've already come up with two lucrative inventions.

Tony gives Alex a scornful look

Sorry—one—if we discount that last failure. Nevertheless, we worked as a team, so give me one really valid reason why I should want you dead? If you come up with another winner, that's even greater fortune for us, and no Dinah to worry about.

Tony remains silent, thinking. Alex picks up the revolver

Would you rather reload the gun yourself? (*He hands Tony the revolver*)

Tony (*taking the gun hesitantly*) What the hell, I'll put my life in your hands and rely on your unwavering affection for me. (*He puts the gun on the coffee table*)

Alex As you wish. (*He checks his watch*) Dinah will arrive soon so I think you ought to make yourself scarce.

Tony Whatever you say. (*He goes towards the french windows*)

Alex And by the way, you're certain you know how to put Dinah's car out of action?

Tony (*stops, turns*) We've been over the moves more times than a grand master. I sabotage the distributor cap, right?

Alex You must make absolutely sure her car won't start because it's the most crucial part of the plan. If that goes wrong we're up the Swanee because there's no other way I can delay her until the fateful hour.

Tony (*as an afterthought*) How do I get to the distributor cap?

Alex (*surprised at the question*) Huh? Pull the bonnet release, lift the—

Tony I mean if she's locked her car?

Alex She never locks her car while it's parked here, and since she's a creature of habit, she won't have changed her routine.

Tony (*persistent*) But if she *has*?

Alex Christ, you're supposed to be the genius—stick a potato up the exhaust.

Tony She won't be able to see me tampering with her car from here, will she?

Alex I've jammed the gate so she'll have to park in the yard.

Tony You've thought of everything, haven't you?

Alex Can't afford any loose ends, can we?

Tony Of course not, so what important matter have you overlooked?

Alex Me?

Tony Think hard, old boy—it's on the props list.

Alex Thank you for reminding me. (*He takes a cigarette lighter from his pocket*) I suppose that with the adrenalin already beginning to flow, I almost forgot, Exhibit "A"—one cigarette lighter (*he flicks it on*)—in working order. (*He goes to the desk and puts the lighter in the top right-hand drawer*)

Tony (*moving nearer the french windows*) I'll stay in the barn until it's time for the action. I have some specifications to check over.

Alex (*closing the drawer and turning*) Goodbye Tony.

Tony opens the french window but the tone of Alex's farewell causes him to hesitate for a moment

Tony Alex . . .

Alex (*moving to the front of the sofa*) Yes?

Tony You don't think we should have changed my name—so that Dinah won't *ever* find out?

Alex Don't worry Tony . . . Dinah won't be seeing you again.

This causes Tony to hesitate again, then he leaves by the french windows, his manner uncertain. He closes the doors, eyes Alex through them for a moment, then moves out of sight left, as

    Cathy comes through the main entrance. She has put on a jacket and is carrying an abstract painting

Cathy What's eating him?

Alex Only a mild attack of stage fright, nothing serious. I suppose he's bound to be a little apprehensive since he thinks I'm going to have him killed.

Cathy (*moving nearer Alex*) Well you are, aren't you?

Alex Don't you start.

Cathy I take it it's all "go" for tonight?

Alex Yes, we "go". You have the flask of blood?

Cathy It's in the spare room.

Alex Good—good, then the trap is neatly baited. All we need now is the big bad mouse. (*Noticing the painting*) What is *that*?

Cathy You know very well it's the painting I've been doing of Colonel Fox-croft. (*She holds it up for Alex to see*) What do you think?

Alex Why it's—it's—what's the word I'm looking for?

Cathy Genius.

Alex Er, no!

Cathy Beast.

Alex Seriously—it is quite superb . . . what *exactly* is it?

Cathy I've called it *Evolution*; it's supposed to depict man's struggle to find himself. (*She hands the painting to Alex*)

Alex (*holding the painting the wrong way round*) Yes, yes, I see.

Cathy You're holding it the wrong way round.

Alex (*turning the picture*) Oh, sorry, couldn't see where you'd signed it. (*He appraises the picture*) And the Colonel's into this sort of thing. (*He rests the picture against the side of the sofa*)

Cathy I'll say! Has a great-nephew or some such relation at art college.

Alex How unusual.

Cathy That he has a great-nephew at art college?

Alex No, that he's a patron of avant-garde. Being a prominent historian I'd have thought the *Charge of the Light Brigade* would be more his scene.

Cathy Whatever turns you on. By the way, you *are* going to sponsor my London Exhibition, aren't you?

Alex I promised I would when my funds flow freely again, didn't I? You know I'm crazy about anything that's tax deductible. It *will* be deductible won't it?

Cathy I guess so. That exhibition could be the big break I'm looking for. Once people recognize my style, discover the hidden message in my pictures—

Alex You mean like "Spot the Ball"?

Cathy You won't sneer at my work when my paintings make you a handsome profit.

Alex Sorry, I spoke tongue-in-cheek, now there's an interesting idea for you to paint. While we're on the subject, I hope I don't have to wait *too* long for a return on my investment, after all, most paintings aren't worth much until *after* the artist's death.

Cathy There you are—the perfect motive for murder.

Alex Yes, an alluring thought, maybe we could fake your death as well, make a double killing so to speak, well, not *exactly* a double killing, if you know what I mean.

Cathy I'm not sure that I do.

Alex Meaning what?

Cathy (*moves past Alex, stops*) Meaning I'm not sure you don't intend to have Tony killed.

Alex (*moving away from Cathy*) Ye gods, why do YOU think that?

Cathy He sounded pret-ty edgy before he left.

Alex I didn't realize you were listening.

Cathy I overheard everything.

Alex (*hesitating*) Everything?

Cathy The salient points.

Alex Hmm, and what conclusion did you reach?

Cathy What conclusion did I need to reach? I always felt it was a viable proposition for you to switch bullets.

Alex (*going nearer to Cathy*) Why would I do that?

Cathy Oh, come on Alex, you don't need me to spell it all out.

Alex Okay, so I have Tony bumped off, Dinah carries the can and I register the patent in my own name. Plausible, possible, but why?

Cathy So that you can extract the revenge on Dinah you've waited so long for.

Alex I'm not so vindictive I'd want to convert Dinah into an unwitting but gen-u-ine murderess.

Cathy (*forcefully*) You loathe her and everything she stands for and nothing would give you greater delight than to see her facing a murder rap, her neck in the noose and her career destroyed.

Alex I've never envied her, nor her success. She writes a pathetic sob column which is of no interest to me whatsoever.

Cathy (*picking up the newspaper*) Then why do you read it every Friday?

Alex I—buy it for the racing tips, not that their selections ever come up.

Cathy (*persistently*) It was open at the "Dear Dinah" page.

Alex Only because I was showing Tony how she starts every reply with "I know exactly how you feel".

Cathy (*throwing the newspaper on the sofa*) You can't fool me. You won't be satisfied until that condemned lady finally mounts the scaffold.

Alex I have no intention of having Dinah shoot Tony for real and the thought never occurred to me.

Cathy That isn't what you told Tony.

Alex You must have been listening intently.

Cathy And come to think, what were you digging near the cliff top?

Alex Me? When?

Cathy Yesterday. I saw you as I walked back from the Iredale's cottage. I had to go for fresh cream.

Alex Oh, yesterday! Yes, I remember. I was digging a burial plot for Tony's body. You know, the guy I'm having shot. It's a nice spot, peaceful, tranquil, and facing the equator. What better send off could—

Cathy I thought it seemed about the right size for that.

Alex Okay, since you've obviously had me under surveillance for the last couple of days, I'd better put your mind at rest. The excavation was merely for the purpose of burying the rubbish left by those awful scouts I foolishly allowed to camp there last weekend. Didn't want to despatch the refuse over the cliff and pollute the ocean.

Cathy Don't tell me you've joined Friends of the Earth.

Alex All right, I won't. (*A pause*) Did you think I would switch the bullets?

Cathy I don't think it would cause you sleepless nights.

Alex For the same motives Tony suggested?

Cathy Of course.

Alex You heard me admit to Tony that the idea had crossed my mind, but why would I kill the goose that lays the golden eggs? How could I possibly benefit? Tony has a brilliant mind and is assured of further success, so I guarantee that after Dinah has killed—I mean shot him—he'll walk out unscathed or at the worst, with a streaming cold if he's been caught out there in the storm.

Cathy (*thinking*) If you had sole rights to his patent—

Alex *Our* patent—I put up all the capital.

Cathy His, yours, what difference? The income from the sole rights would be at least a million in the first year—

Alex I thought you were supposed to be an artist not a cost accountant—

Cathy The income from just one patent would be quite sufficient for you—you'd have no further need for Tony. (*Pauses*) I could benefit also.

Alex (*astonished*) Am I to understand that you *do* want me to switch bullets and have Dinah kill Tony?

Cathy The motive is obvious, the opportunity ideal.

Alex (*thinking*) I'm not sure Dinah is all that good a shot. (*He heads for the buffet*)

Cathy Surely not even Dinah could miss from point-blank range.

Alex (*mixing something*) You, for your part would want a larger slice of the cake, a more generous share of the spoils?

Cathy Naturally we'd take a split. I could use the extra cash to exhibit my works in Paris and New York.

Alex moves towards Cathy, taking a swig of his drink

You drink too much.

Alex In times of decision a man and his scotch should be seldom parted.

Cathy You'll do it then?

Alex It's an attractive proposition.

Cathy Yes or no? I need to know the score.

Alex (*considering his drink, or what's left of it*) You don't like Tony, do you?

Cathy He's a fag for Chrissakes, a real weirdo. I always have an uneasy feeling when he's around. I don't quite know what it is—a strange kind of tension. Personally, I don't think he's all there—

Alex Yes, well they say it's a thin line which divides genius from madman.

Cathy And he's thus totally expendable?

Alex finishes his drink with one triumphant gesture and puts the glass on the coffee table fiercely

Alex Very well, I'll do it!

Cathy (*uncertainly*) Seriously?

Alex Goddammit, yes! I'll do it. I won't have had so much fun since Dinah called the fuzz to have them arrest the radio! (*He stops, thinks*) There is, unfortunately, one small problem.

Cathy Which is?

Alex How can I be assured of your *complete* discretion?

Cathy If you can't trust me now, I don't know what.

Alex (*moving nearer the desk*) As you said, you'd know the whole score and that would leave me open to blackmail.

Cathy moves towards Alex and is about to correct him

Alternatively, you might turn Queen's evidence and reach a deal with Dinah. Freed from jail, she'd have her story of a lifetime. "Writer of the Year", paperback rights, film rights and all that jazz, while I sit it out on Murderer's Row—a sad and depressing finale for me. (*A moment's thought*) There's only *one* way I can be sure of your total silence.

Cathy Don't be an idiot, I would never—

Alex Bury you with the empty cans and wrappings in the grave I prepared for Tony—

Cathy (*a little frightened*) Don't talk like that!

Alex *Or* I could hurl you over the cliff like a rag doll—the water is deep enough. What's it to be?

Cathy (*now genuinely frightened*) Alex, for God's sake—

She turns away from Alex, and as she does so, Alex whips up the paper-knife from the desk, grabs Cathy round the neck and pretends to stab her in the back with the knife

Alex A knife in the back?

Cathy (*freeing herself*) Alex, please!

Alex (*replacing the knife on the desk, moving after Cathy*) No a knife's too messy—blood all over the place. (*Looking about the sofa*) I know, the cushion method! (*He picks up the cushion and holds it in both hands*) Much cleaner, and I won't be able to hear your pitiful screams!

Cathy is frozen in terror, and Alex suddenly collapses on the sofa in a fit of laughter

You thought I'd do it! You really thought I'd do it!

Cathy (*with obvious relief*) Don't you *ever* play a joke like that on me again!

Alex (*replacing the cushion*) And you thought I'd go along with your plea to have Tony returned to his maker. (*Rising*) I didn't know there was a ghoulish streak in your nature. (*He rests his hands on Cathy's shoulders*) I'm sorry if I frightened you just now, but it was *you* who raised the subject of murder. I am a man of integrity and honour who would *never* cheat on his partner. Neither would I kill you, because I need you for tonight's gala performance, don't I?

Cathy nods agreement

Now, didn't you mention something about an appointment with Colonel Foxcroft? I don't want you here when Dinah arrives.

Cathy (*moving away*) Yes, I'd better go while I'm still relatively intact. You had me real scared then—I guess it's all those detective thrillers you read.

Alex You're probably right—I can't resist the occasional urge to act the part of one of my favourite villains.

Cathy I guess I'll be gone maybe a couple of hours. (*She checks her watch*) Back around seven. (*She collects the painting and goes to the main entrance*)

Alex Remember me to the Colonel—in fact, ask him to pop over for a drink some time. We can talk about the war.

Cathy Sure thing. (*She starts to exit, then turns*) Alex—it is a good idea, isn't it?

Alex What is?

Cathy . . . switching the bullets.

Alex (*thoughtfully*) Yes, it is . . .

Cathy exits

(*Picking up the gun; considering it*) . . . it certainly is . . .

Alex is contemplating possibilities as the lights fade to—

Black-out

SCENE 2

The same. Later that evening

When the lights come up, Alex is pacing about the room, drink in hand. He is obviously restless and impatient. Understandable; time is getting on and there is no sign of Dinah. He glances at his watch, frowns, and goes over to the french windows to look out. Still no Dinah! Where is she, for heaven's sake? Over to the sofa, sits down. A swig of his drink, another glance at his watch and the waiting now almost unbearable. He puts his glass on the coffee table. Decision time. Call her office? Find out what has happened? He goes over to the telephone and dials a London (ten-digit) number

Alex (*when the connection has been made*) Put me through to Dinah Conrad's office please . . . would you check anyway? . . . *Mr Conrad* . . . When did

she leave? ... Did she leave a message to say where she was going? ...
No. It doesn't matter. Thank you. (*Replacing the receiver*) Damn that woman.

A taxi pulls up outside. Alex quickly finishes his drink, and with renewed enthusiasm hurries to the french windows to look out again, then turns

Dinah walks swiftly into the room from UR. She is an imposing woman, about the same age as Alex, and is wearing a tweed coat with matching shoulder bag, over a smart two-piece. Her very presence seems to radiate command and authority

I'd all but given you up.

Dinah Pay the taxi driver please, Alex.

Alex (*stunned*) Taxi driver?

Dinah (*moving DC*) I'll explain later, just pay him, will you—and give him a decent gratuity, he's been most helpful.

This unexpected development leaves Alex speechless. Dinah has only just arrived and already the first part of the plan is in ruins

Alex exits

Dinah throws her shoulder bag on to the sofa and gives the room a quick appraisal

Alex (*off*) How much on the meter?

Taxi Driver (*off*) Seven pounds forty sir.

Alex (*off*) There—and er—keep the change.

Taxi Driver (*off*) Thank *you* sir, I'm obliged.

Alex returns

Dinah, who has cast her expert eye over the paintings, looks disapprovingly at the one above the desk

Dinah Jesus wept!

Alex (*moving to the far side of the sofa, away from Dinah*) What's gone wrong—I mean, what's happened?

Dinah (*still occupied with the painting*) Where *did* you acquire these awful paintings?

Alex (*ignoring the question*) Why the taxi—where's your car? (*He notices Dinah's shoulder bag on the sofa*)

Dinah (*turning to face the painting above the hi-fi*) They make the room feel so—oppressive.

The taxi pulls away

Alex Dinah, I've been worried about you. I've just rung your office to find out where you were.

Dinah (*sternly*) Why did you have to ring my office? You knew I was coming.

Alex Don't fret, I only got as far as the switchboard, so I didn't have chance to be offensive to your devoted secretary.

Dinah (*more at ease*) That's a relief.

Alex (*moving to the front of the sofa*) So, why did you have to hire a taxi? Where's your car?

Dinah Broke down outside the village, had to be towed to the garage where it will be for God knows how long. What a day I've had. First, no alarm call, so I'm caught in the traffic chaos caused by the damned tube strike—*that* makes me late for a literary luncheon, *then* my editor has been hounding me all day for copy to beat the deadline, and to seal everything, my car splutters to a complete stop. Sometimes I wonder if the price of success is worthwhile after all.

Alex Become a missionary—at least you'd be doing more good than harm.

Dinah gives Alex a hostile glare. She's probably used to this type of banter but nevertheless finds Alex tiresome. She takes off her coat to hand it to Alex, who makes no attempt to take it

I've reserved your usual coat hook.

Dinah (*firmly*) I see your hospitality still doesn't extend to courtesy.

Alex I'm still the ignoramus you deserted three years ago.

Dinah exits UR to hang up her coat

Alex snatches up Dinah's shoulder bag, opens it and takes out her cigarette lighter. He closes the bag, puts it back on the sofa, then checks the lighter is working, for no apparent reason other than habit, before putting it in his jacket pocket

Dinah enters

Dinah If it hadn't been for that kind taxi driver, I don't know what I'd have done.

Alex That kind taxi driver has just set me back a tenner. I was going to put that on 'Loop the Loop' in the three-thirty tomorrow.

Dinah I told you to tip him, not give him an annuity.

Alex (*changing the subject*) When will your car be ready?

Dinah Lunchtime tomorrow at the earliest. (*She sinks on to the sofa*) God I'm exhausted.(*She stretches her legs*)

Alex Shall I ring the garage and ask if they can attend to it straight away?

Dinah (*wearily*) There's no point—they were just closing for the day when we got there. If I'd broken down an hour earlier I might just have made it.

Alex Hmm, most unfortunate. (*Pacing the room, thinking things out. He may be able to retrieve the situation after all*) How are you going to get home tonight?

Dinah I don't see how I can unless you'll take me.

Alex (*at the back of the sofa*) I can't—I'm expecting Cathy back any minute and we were going to have a—quiet evening together.

Dinah I realize it would be terribly inconvenient for you, but I do have an important appointment in the morning.

Alex Dinah, if I'd nothing doing tonight I'd willingly drive you home, but I'm a little tired and under the weather, and don't really feel up to it. That leaves us with the problem of where you're going to stay tonight.

Dinah (*rising, turning*) Here, of course.

Alex Here? (*Moving round to front of sofa*) You can't. As I said, I'm expecting Cathy—

Dinah And I'd be in the way?

Alex It could be embarrassing for all of us.

Dinah (*thinking*) I see. Where do you suggest I stay tonight then?

Alex There's the hotel in the village.

Dinah It's a cold, draughty place.

Alex You'd get a special rate as it's the weekend.

Dinah Alex, I don't want to be alone tonight. There's a storm forecast, and you know how thunder frightens me.

Alex There'll be other guests there.

Dinah I don't have any luggage—if I check in without any they might think I'm a—hooker.

Alex (*teasingly*) Surely not.

Dinah (*with a scornful look*) You're not remotely amusing, Alex. Look I could stay here while you and Katie—

Alex Cathy—

Dinah You and Cathy could stay at the hotel.

Alex Return to find you've claimed squatters rights? And I thought you said you didn't want to be alone tonight.

Dinah God, you are so pathetic. (*Heading for the desk*) I suppose I'll have to stay at the hotel. (*She lifts the telephone receiver*)

Alex (*moving after her*) Who are you going to call?

Dinah (*starting to dial*) The hotel. I'd better make a reservation.

Alex (*putting his hand over the telephone to cut off the call*) All right, you can stay here tonight, okay?

Dinah (*replacing the receiver*) That's most considerate of you.

Alex (*moving to the coffee table*) I'm going to mix myself a drink. (*He collects his empty glass*) Can I get you anything? (*He heads for the buffet*)

Dinah Whatever you're having—on the rocks.

Alex Ice as well?

Dinah (*moving to the sofa*) Now, tell me what is so important you couldn't discuss it over the 'phone. I assume you didn't ask me down here just to fix the TV.

Alex (*pouring his drink*) It's a rather delicate matter—

Dinah I thought as much, Forget the drink, I'd prefer to remain sober for the moment.

Alex comes downstage with his drink, takes a hesitant sip

Go on then, tell me all. Elucidate upon your problem. (*She sits down on the sofa*)

Alex (*coming to the front of the sofa*) I feared that had I 'phoned, we'd have had another of our heated arguments, and as you're so fond of the cottage, I thought it a good idea if you came here for a friendly discussion, man to beast.

Dinah The cottage is *the* one thing about you I do approve of. The peace and isolation is something of a tonic after a week of slavery on Fleet Street. This is almost paradise in comparison.

Alex Thank you for the travelogue, but I fear this isolated paradise will be mine no longer unless you agree to re-negotiate the settlement. I'll have to move into a bed-sit.

Dinah My wildest suspicion *is* confirmed—you *do* want to discuss dollars and cents.

Alex Your enthusiasm overwhelms me but please—hear me out. (*A pause for thought*) The thing is, due to the alarming ineptitude of those in whom I misguidedly placed my financial trust, the unwillingness of my bank manager to extend my credit *and* allow a moratorium in respect of past expenditure incurred, particularly in relation to our matrimonial differences, and the intolerant attitude of local traders, most notably Messrs Ladbrokes, I find myself in an unenviable state of flux, *vis à vis* my cash-flow situation, despite the most strenuous efforts on my part to extricate myself from this unfortunate predicament—

Dinah (*yawning—she has heard all this before*) Sorry Alex, what was that?

Alex (*sadly*) I'm almost broke, Frankly, after I've paid your allowance, I'm left with very little on which to survive. I admit the fault is *partly* mine, but as you are aware, my only other income is from my trust fund.

Dinah (*rising*) Why should I suffer because of your shady deals? Even I could have advised you not to squander your money on that painter friend of yours—it must be costing you a fortune to continue that frivolous affair.

Alex I'm not having an affair, I'm having a relationship, and when I need *your* advice, I'll write to you. My money has gone elsewhere. I backed Tony in a venture which failed to yield the expected return—failed to yield *any* return, in fact.

Dinah So you need me to bail you out?

Alex We thought we were on to something big—a real winner, but we were beaten to the market with the patent. Some consortium was working on the same idea.

Dinah It happens—you win some, you lose some. Now you need Tony to come up with another lucrative invention?

Alex Exactly, but he's suffering from inventor's cramp at the moment.

Dinah Don't despair, the great mind may strike at any moment. What puzzles me is why this—Tony—needs your help. Didn't you tell me he came from a wealthy family? If that's right, why can't he launch his ideas himself? Why does he have to come running to you?

Alex He's completely lacking in business sense, so his family won't give him the necessary finance. He doesn't know how to choose the right options or make the best deals—the City financiers would take him to the cleaners. You have to be ruthless in today's business world.

Dinah That's where you come in, the ruthless half of the partnership?

Alex I wouldn't put it quite like that. I provide the finance for his research and arrange the best deal.

He sips his drink, Dinah remains silent

I take it your silence indicates agreement? You'll take a reduction until my situation improves?

Dinah I will not! This is not the first time you've tried to dishonour your commitments. What was it the last time . . . your bank manager cancelled your weekly golf match because you were overdrawn? I'm a little older and a little wiser to your tricks, and I suspect you've got some kind of deal lined up—I don't know what it is and I don't wish to know, but I'm sorry Alex, your request is declined. (*A pause*) Anyway, I'm having the flat completely redecorated, so I need the money.

Alex (*pleading*) But Dinah, you're earning a fortune—I'm on the breadline.

Dinah (*glancing round the room*) Yes, there certainly is an air of poverty about the place. I see the walls peeling, the ceiling crumbling. (*Motioning towards the buffet*) But at least you're not short of liquid assets.

Alex You've made your point.

Dinah Why don't you sell off a few family heirlooms to tide you over?

Alex (*resentfully*) Because you'd get half the proceeds. (*He finishes his drink as if by way of protest*)

Dinah That's right, under the terms of the settlement, half your income from whatever the source.

Alex (*heading for the buffet with his empty glass*) You heartless predator! You Jezebel! (*He puts his empty glass on the buffet*)

Dinah Flattery will not change my mind.

Alex (*moving back downstage*) That's your final decision then?

Dinah Yes Alex, I'm afraid it is.

Alex (*trying another angle*) Any chance of your marrying that guy you've been seeing lately?

Dinah (*surprised*) You—know about Julian?

Alex (*chuckling to himself*) I didn't know his name was Julian. What is he—the ladies' fashion editor?

Dinah Have you had a private detective checking up on me?

Alex Yeh, I hired Philip Marlow at twenty dollars a day plus expenses.

Dinah How did you find out about Julian?

Alex Hetty said she saw you with a gentleman of uncertain ancestry in a restaurant you recommended—the "Blue Pagoda" I think she said it was called—last time she was in town.

Dinah Actually, it's called the "Green Pagoda". And Hetty ought to mind her own damned business.

Alex Hetty said she was too embarrassed to say "hello". I must say he sounded a real wimp when he answered your 'phone. "Hi, Dinah Conrad's apartment, can I help you?" I thought I'd dialled Gay Lib by mistake. Is it serious?

Dinah He's nothing more than a close friend, so don't get excited, because you're not going to get out of paying my allowance *that* way.

Alex If you must have an affair with some bionic beanpole—

Dinah I'm not having an affair . . . I'm having a relationship.

Alex Please keep it a little less public. What *must* Hetty think?

Dinah I couldn't care less what Hetty thinks.

Alex I might just pop in to the "Green Pagoda" sometime and look Julian over—is he gay?

Dinah Eccentric but harmless.

Alex (*complaining*) Isn't it enough that you humiliate me every week in your column? (*He picks up the newspaper and points aggressively at it*) "I know exactly how you feel". (*He puts the newspaper down*)

Dinah How on earth can that humiliate you?

Alex It's your weekly stab at me. You know the symptoms—you experienced them all with me. I don't like it.

Dinah I do believe you have developed an inferiority complex. Fancy that! I'm not having a "weekly stab" at you at all. I must identify myself with the reader's problem, so "I know exactly how you feel" is my catchphrase.

Alex Dinah "I know exactly how you feel" Conrad? I'd feel a little more secure if your paper made you their "Far East correspondent".

Dinah I didn't come here for a career assessment, I came to discuss "certain financial matters". Which reminds me, I haven't received last month's cheque yet.

Alex No!

Dinah It's not the first time you've missed either.

Alex I keep an accurate record in my files and I distinctly remember posting it—I'll check with the bank first thing Monday morning.

Dinah You'd better, otherwise I'll have my solicitor write to you again.

Alex That won't be necessary.

Dinah God, how you exasperate me. (*She picks up her shoulder bag, opens it and takes out a packet of cigarettes*) Why is it that whenever I've spoken with you or seen you, I notice new grey hairs? (*She rummages in her bag for her cigarette lighter*) Funny, I could have sworn—I must have left my lighter in the office. (*She puts her bag back on the sofa*) May I use yours, or have you given them up?

Alex I've packed them in. Cathy convinced me I'd live longer.

Dinah How did she manage to succeed where so many others have failed?

Alex She can be very—persuasive. My old lighter is in the desk drawer.

Seeing that Alex isn't going to get the lighter, Dinah goes over to the desk, followed by Alex, and opens the middle drawer of the desk

No, top right, I think.

Dinah opens the top right-hand drawer, sees the revolver and takes it out, unintentionally aiming it at Alex, who lapses into the mode of a terrified victim and raises both hands

Don't shoot, for God's sake Dinah, don't shoot! I'll write you a cheque now but *please*, hold your fire!

Dinah (*totally unmoved*) What is this for?

Alex (*himself again*) It's a trick lighter. You aim the barrel towards yourself, squeeze the trigger and presto, your cigarette lights up.

Dinah Last of the funny men, aren't you? Why the gun?

Alex (*going to the front of the sofa*) For protection, why do you think? The house is stocked with priceless paintings and valuable books, so I need it to help deter pillagers and any other unsavoury characters who might get ideas.

Dinah is tapping the gun in her hand

Hey, don't toy with that thing, it's loaded.

Dinah replaces the gun in the drawer and takes out the cigarette lighter

Then there's the prowler.

Dinah (*moving nearer coffee table*) Prowler? (*She lights a cigarette and puts the lighter on the coffee table*)

Alex Prowler, tramp, whatever you call them. Been hanging around the area—caused havoc in the Iredales' chicken hut. I've informed the police but I don't think they've caught anyone yet.

Dinah What would a prowler want with those appalling paintings?

Alex (*sternly*) They are works of art!

Dinah Since when did *you* know anything about art? You're just saying that because Katie painted them.

Alex Cathy—her name is Cathy.

Dinah Do you want my opinion?

Alex Not really, but I've a feeling I'm going to get it.

Dinah She's not a very creative painter.

Alex She's not a painter. (*Proudly*) She's an artist!

Dinah No kidding? For God's sake don't let her paint the bathroom! (*After a deep drag on her cigarette*) What's for dinner? I assume there is *some* food in the house, or do you have to rely on Meals on Wheels?

Alex Cathy's made a meatloaf. There may be enough for three.

Dinah Meatloaf? Yuk, you know I hate meatloaf.

Alex I'm sorry if the bill of fayre doesn't appeal to you, but we didn't expect you for dinner. Had I known, I'd have defrosted a mallard and ordered a crate of Moët and Chandon. You'll adore Cathy's meatloaf—she's a marvellous cook.

Dinah If her cooking is anything like her painting. I'll settle for a glass of milk and a biscuit.

Alex Tell you what—we'll celebrate tonight. I'll open a bottle of vintage vino. It'll help kill the taste of her meatloaf.

Dinah Then Cathy's *not* all that good a hostess?

Alex To be perfectly frank, she ought to stick with oils and canvas. Be honest—do I appear neglected?

Dinah I'm sure your affair has other advantages.

A van pulls up outside

Alex That's probably Cathy.

A grinding of gears

That *is* Cathy.

Dinah stubs out her cigarette in the ash tray on the coffee table

Please, no scenes, let's just have a nice quiet evening together. We can sit round the fireside and sing songs.

Dinah (*picking up the cigarette lighter*) You two can sing what you want, but I'll curl up with a book. (*She goes to the desk and puts the lighter back in the drawer*)

Cathy enters

Cathy (*not seeing Dinah at first*) Hi, isn't the Agony Aunt here yet? I don't see her car in— (*she sees Dinah*) Oh, I'm sorry, I guess I've made a real lulu of myself.

Dinah (*moving to the front of the sofa*) I guess you're used to it.

Alex (*moving towards Cathy*) Cathy—Dinah. Dinah—Cathy.

Cathy (*moving past Alex towards Dinah*) I guess I'd better start again. Hi, Mrs Conrad.

Dinah (*sternly*) Hello Cathy, and please—call me Dinah. Alex has spoken so much about you, but I expected someone a little—older.

Cathy Alex has told me so much about you. (*Admiring Dinah's two-piece*) I must say, I like your outfit. You have excellent taste.

Dinah Thank you.

Cathy The Empire's not dead yet.

Dinah gives Cathy a basilisk stare

Alex (*to Cathy, before Dinah can retort*) We have ourselves a bit of a problem. Dinah's car has broken down and it won't be ready until tomorrow—

Cathy Oh, that explains why—

Alex (*quickly*) Quite, so Dinah's staying here for the night.

Cathy That will be nice.

Alex (*quickly again*) Now that you're introduced, how about cocktails before dinner?

Cathy Bourbon.

Alex Dinah?

Dinah I would like a dry sherry please, Alex.

Alex Splendid. (*He goes to the buffet*) I won't say no to a little snifter myself. (*He starts mixing the drinks*)

Dinah You never say no to a little snifter. (*To Cathy*) You *are* aware my husband is an incipient alcoholic?

Cathy I keep telling him he drinks too much, but he has cut down lately.

Dinah I'm pleased to hear he's finally taken someone's advice—he never took mine.

Alex (*turning*) That's because you never gave me any. You didn't even print my letter.

Dinah *Your* letter?

Alex Yes, I wrote to the "Dear Dinah" column, signed myself "Shy and Reserved of Newport Pagnell". (*He approaches them with the drinks*)

Dinah That is the sort of childish trick you would play. It's a great pity you have nothing better to do with your time, because all crank mail goes straight into the waste-bin.

Alex (*handing out the drinks*) One bourbon, one dry sherry. (*He raises his glass in a toast*) Cheers, let us eat, drink and be merry, for tomorrow we all die! *Ten Little Indians*, Act One Scene One—no, I tell a lie, Act One Scene *Two*.

Dinah (*to Cathy*) Ignore him, he has an acid sense of humour.

Cathy He's quite amusing once you've got used to him.

Dinah And you've got used to him? Isn't he a little elderly to be your lover?

Cathy I look upon him more as—a father figure, rather than a lover . . .

Alex whimpers and turns away, obviously hurt

... but I guess I see a different side of him. He's helped me tremendously with my career and has been most generous.

Dinah Generous? Alex? (*She laughs*) I found generosity to be the least of his attributes. I rather found him selfish, intolerant, offensive—

Cathy Mrs Conrad—

Alex Let her finish—those are my good points.

Dinah Glib, superficial.

Cathy You obviously have a lot in common.

Alex I may not have been the perfect husband, but since I started to read your column I've improved enormously. (*To Cathy*) Haven't I?

Cathy Yes, you have.

Alex How did the Colonel like your painting?

Cathy He was understandably impressed and I got myself a sale.

Dinah (*to Cathy*) God, you don't actually let those pictures out of the house, do you?

Alex (*to Dinah*) Cathy is a talented abstract painter—

Cathy I'm an artist, not a painter!

Alex I'm convinced she has a promising career ahead of her—that's why I've bought some of her pictures. They'll be valuable in a few years time.

Dinah Praise indeed from someone who couldn't tell a Rembrandt from a Turner, a Constable from—

Alex I think we get the gist.

Dinah (*to Cathy*) Is abstract work *all* you do?

Cathy I do some portrait work.

Dinah Really?

Alex (*proudly*) Cathy has promised to paint *my* portrait.

Dinah (*to Cathy*) You specialize in still-life as well then?

Alex (*to Dinah*) Please don't joke like that, Dinah. I'm sure Cathy doesn't want to hear your witticisms all night.

Dinah Whatever happened to your sense of humour? (*To Cathy*) Honestly Cathy, I wish you every success in your career. As you may know, under the terms of the divorce settlement, Alex must pay me half of his income, so the more successful you are, all the better for me.

Alex (*to Dinah*) If you're through with your budget, perhaps we ought to organize the accommodation for tonight. You can have the spare room down here and Cathy and I will share the bridal suite.

Dinah *You will not!* No way do you sleep with Cathy while I'm here, show me that much respect at least.

Alex For God's sake Dinah, we're all adults. The double bed doesn't creak any more, so you won't be disturbed.

Dinah I know I won't be disturbed. *You* will have the large bedroom, I'll have the small one. If that prowler is still on the loose, I'll feel much safer upstairs.

Cathy Prowler?

Alex You know—last week.

Cathy Oh *that*, Yes, Alex reported it to the police, but we haven't heard anything from them yet.

Dinah Yes, Alex was saying.

Alex I should think the sight of Dinah in her nightie will be enough to scare any prowler into the next county.

Dinah What did you say about uncalled-for witticisms? (*To Cathy*) Will you make up a bed in the spare room down here for yourself?

Cathy (*resignedly*) I guess so.

Dinah Why do you Americans always have to answer a question with "I guess so"?

Cathy I guess it's because—oh there I go again!

Dinah (*to Alex*) Do we take it our esteemed host is satisfied with the arrangements?

Alex I guess so—yes.

Dinah (*with a sly smile*) I'm so glad. (*To Cathy*) Have you a spare nightdress I could use? I don't have any luggage with me.

Cathy I think I'm a few sizes smaller than you, but I'll see what I can find.

Dinah Boy, I can see we're in for a long tedious evening.

Cathy Oh, I don't know, I'm sure we'll be able to liven it up somehow.

Alex gives Cathy a discerning stare as the Lights fade to—

Black-out

SCENE 3

The same, about three hours later

When the lights come up, Dinah is seated on the sofa, absorbed in a book. The curtains at the french windows are drawn and the room's lamps are lighted.

After a moment, Alex comes in through the main entrance and heads straight for the buffet

Alex (*mixing a drink*) You could have helped Cathy clear the things away.

Dinah (*looking up from her book*) I'm a guest here, so I'm not expected to help with the housework. Besides, I'm still recovering from that awful meatloaf. I'm warning you Alex, any permanent damage and I'll sue.

Alex (*turning with his drink*) Her cooking isn't *that* bad.

Dinah Not bad? She can't even make a decent cup of tea.

Alex (*moving to rear of the sofa*) What was wrong with her tea?

Dinah It wasn't even coloured. Why don't you go help Cathy finish in the kitchen?

Alex You know how clumsy I am with dishes, and she's nearly through now. Would you like a drink?

Dinah No thank you, and *please* don't distract me—I'm trying to read.

Alex Sorry. (*He sips his drink*) Good book?

Dinah Hmm?

Alex I asked if it is a good book.

Dinah So-so.

Alex Anything interesting?

Dinah (*annoyed at Alex's persistence*) A rather boring thriller if you *must* know.

Alex (*moving round to front of sofa*) Didn't think you were in to thrillers. (*He sips his drink*)

Dinah I'm not but it's all you seem to have.

Alex You know I like mysteries. What is it then, *Poirot Investigates*? (*He sips his drink again*)

Dinah (*clearly annoyed; scanning the cover*) *Calibre*.

Alex (*spluttering his drink*) Jesus Christmas!

Dinah I beg your pardon?

Alex (*pointing to his glass*) Strong stuff, nearly choked me.

Dinah You're determined to get drunk tonight, aren't you?

Alex Can you give me one good reason why I shouldn't?

Dinah remains silent and resumes reading; Alex is clearly concerned about the situation

Why did you choose that book in particular?

Dinah looks up again; it is clear she is not going to progress much further at the moment

Dinah What *is* the matter with you? You *do* keep all your books in strict alphabetical order, don't you? (*She reads the cover again*) *Calibre*, by Edward Chesney Abcot, happened to be the first book on the shelf.

Alex (*putting his glass on the coffee table*) How far have you got?

Dinah What *is* bothering you? You've seemed restless all evening.

Alex Just the excitement of having you here. Where have you got to?

Dinah (*checking the page*) Eleanor has arrived at the hunting lodge.

Alex (*turning away relieved*) Thank God for that.

Dinah That Eleanor's arrived at the hunting lodge?

Alex No, that you've only just started the book. I wouldn't bother reading any further, it's a very dull plot.

Dinah I don't like to leave off once I've started.

Alex ... Very disappointing ending—you'll never work out who did it—new character introduced on the final page.

Dinah (*rising*) You're determined to spoil this for me, aren't you? (*Closing the book*) There's little point my continuing, so you might as well tell me how it ends.

Alex The butler did it.

Dinah How *very* original. (*She puts the book on the coffee table*)

Cathy enters, she has changed into a dazzling lounge suit—in competition with Dinah

Cathy Hi, you two. Doing anything exciting?

Dinah I was trying to read.

Cathy Anything interesting?

Dinah Only one of Alex's thrillers. (*She picks up the book to check the title again*) *Calibre*.

Cathy (*stopping*) Oh my God!

Dinah (*moving to the bookshelf*) What *is* the matter with you both? (*Replacing* *the book on the shelf*) He's been agitated all evening and now *you* seem tense and nervous.

Alex (*to Cathy, quickly*) I was just explaining to Dinah how it ended, seeing how she wouldn't have time to finish it tonight.

Cathy (*approaching Alex*) How it *ended*?

Alex (*realizing Cathy's concern*) You remember—that awful ending where the butler did it. Poison in the Brown Windsor Soup.

Cathy (*relieved*) I don't think I recall that one. (*To Dinah*) He has so many thrillers I lose track of them all. (*She sits down in the swivel chair*)

Dinah (*moving back to the front of the sofa*) I don't know why you're both so concerned about my reading some second-rate thriller.

Cathy It's not that—we just assumed you'd want to join in the fun with us.

Alex Yes, I thought maybe we could play "Monopoly", or something.

Dinah Count me out. (*To Cathy*) Alex *always* gets Park Lane and Mayfair and breaks the bank. I doubt we'd be through much before breakfast.

Alex How does "Happy Families" grab you?

Dinah It doesn't.

Cathy (*to Dinah*) Thought that would be right up your street, Dinah.

Dinah I can do without your cynicism, dear.

Alex (*pacing across the room*) I know, let's play "Reincarnation".

Cathy What's that?

Alex We each have to guess what the other person was on their previous visit to planet earth—with supporting reasons of course.

Dinah How positively gruesome.

Alex (*moving rear of sofa*) I'll start. Cathy, if you think I'm wrong, you can challenge me and each time you successfully challenge me, I have to down a straight scotch. Now in her previous world, I suggest Dinah was a—

Dinah *Alex*, you are utterly ridiculous and totally objectionable. If you both want to play this weird game, go ahead, but without me.

Alex (*sulkily*) Spoil sport.

Dinah (*to Alex*) And I think you've already had far too much to drink for one night. Go sober up.

Cathy I have to agree with Dinah—go sleep it off.

Alex (*moving round to the front of the sofa*) What's this, a conspiracy to deny me my *one* pleasure in life? (*He picks up his glass from the coffee table and looks pleadingly at Dinah*) Just this for the road?

Dinah Finish your drink and call that it for tonight.

Alex finishes his drink in one savouring moment, then turns to Cathy

Alex What are you going to do?

Cathy I think I'll turn in, it's been a hectic day one way or another.

Alex (*to Dinah*) And you, my thorn between two roses?

Dinah I have some letters to write.

Cathy (*moving towards the spare room*) I'll say goodnight.

Dinah Goodnight Cathy, I suppose I'll see you in the morning.

Alex (*to Cathy*) I'll be down later when the coast is clear!

Cathy No, you won't—you'll just have to exercise enormous self-control for once.

Cathy exits

Alex Well that's killed a good weekend.

Dinah Alex, there is a saying that as men grow older, they mature. Why does it have to be the opposite with you?

Alex I don't know—I suppose it's just that I'm playful.

Dinah Remind me to buy you a bone.

Alex Good one Dinah, good one—you're in sparkling form tonight. (*He checks his watch and yawns*) I think I'll hit the sack as well, I'm beginning to feel unusually tired. Must have been something Cathy put in the meatloaf.

Dinah Have you some notepaper I can use?

Alex (*yawning again*) There's writing paper and envelopes in the middle drawer.

Dinah goes to the desk, sits in the swivel chair and opens the drawer, taking out notepaper and envelopes. Alex goes to the french windows. Dinah selects some notepaper; Alex parts the curtains at the french windows—the signal for Tony—and pulls them together again

The storm clouds are certainly gathering—we're in for one helluva downpour tonight. (*He goes to the bottom of the staircase, and turns off the lights, leaving the staircase and desk lights on*) Oh, sorry—can you see all right?

Dinah There's enough light from the desk lamp.

Alex (*yawning*) I'll say goodnight then.

Dinah Goodnight Alex.

Alex starts to climb the staircase

Oh, Alex.

Alex (*stopping*) What now?

Dinah I almost forgot—could I borrow a pair of your pyjamas?

Alex Didn't anything of Cathy's fit?

Dinah (*hesitating*) She's a size smaller than me.

Alex I'll leave my Kung Fu Specials on your bed.

Dinah Don't you have any Disney characters?

Alex (*going up the staircase*) Goodnight Dinah.

Alex exits

Dinah finds a pen in the middle drawer of the desk and starts to write a letter, but finds that the pen has run out of ink. She goes to the sofa and takes her own out of her bag, then returns to the desk and resumes writing. All is calm, then after a few more moments, the sound of the sea can be heard and the curtains at the french windows blow in. Dinah turns, but as she does so, the sound ceases and the curtains settle. Satisfied that nothing is wrong, she continues writing. Everything seems calm again, then Tony steps into the room from between the curtains. He is dressed in the same dark clothes he was wearing earlier and is holding what appears to be a thick length of wood, rather like a log. He moves around the sofa towards Dinah, his movements mildly menacing. Dinah, suddenly sensing someone in the room, turns quickly, sees Tony, and stares at him transfixed for a moment. Tony continues towards her. Dinah is now terrified and whimpers—

Dinah No! . . . no!

Tony makes a gesture at Dinah with the "log": he could be trying to indicate that she has nothing to be afraid of, but she doesn't seem to notice and, unable to hide her fear, she quickly opens the desk drawer; pulls out the gun and shoots Tony, who jerks backwards, dropping the "log", his face a contorted combination of surprise and terror, almost asking "why"? He slumps to the floor between the sofa and the coffee table, surely and obviously dead. Dinah is now hysterical—

Alex! Alex! Oh my God! Alex!

Cathy rushes in from the spare room as Dinah drops the gun; Alex comes pounding down the staircase

Alex ⎤ *(together)* Dinah, what's happened?
Cathy ⎦ Dinah, what is it? *(Seeing a body on the floor)* Oh sweet Jesus! *(She covers her face in shock)*

Alex moves quickly downstage and glances at the body, but in the poor light is unable to identify the victim

Alex *(to Cathy)* Put the lights on Cathy.

Cathy remains in her state of shock

Cathy, the—oh, never mind. *(He moves quickly to the standard lamp, switches it on and glares at Dinah)* What the hell happened, for God's sake?
Dinah *(softly, frozen in the horror of the moment)* He was going to kill me.
Alex *(moving towards Dinah)* What?
Dinah *(a little firmer)* He was going to kill me!
Alex *(making an inspection of the body, discovering the identity)* My God. Dinah! *(Rising slowly)* You've shot Tony!
Dinah *(whimpering)* T-Tony?
Alex *(bending down to check the body again, then rising in grief)* He—he's dead.
Cathy *(coming to the front of the sofa)* Dead? . . . Tony?
Alex *(as much to himself)* Please somebody—tell me I'm dreaming a Vincent Price movie! *(Turning to face Dinah)* What happened, for Christsakes?

Dinah slumps on to the chair, not answering. Alex approaches her and gently grabs her shoulders

Dinah, will you *please* tell me what this is all about? *(He releases her)*
Dinah He was going to attack me.
Alex *(puzzled)* Attack you? How?
Dinah With a length of wood—a log. *(She indicates the "log")*
Alex *(deliberately looking in the wrong direction)* Log? What log? Dinah, you're not making any sense. *(To Cathy)* Did you see what happened?
Cathy I heard a shot, rushed straight in and saw Dinah with the gun, then she dropped it.
Dinah *(mumbling)* He was going to attack me . . . Look, there's the log. *(She points to the floor where Tony has dropped the "log")*

Alex (*picking up the "log"*) *This* isn't a log. (*He unrolls the papers and inspects them*) It's a set of plans.

Dinah He was attacking me with them.

Alex Attacking you?

Dinah (*hesitating*) Well—he was about to.

Alex (*to Cathy*) Did you see Tony about to attack Dinah?

Cathy (*after a pause*) No, I didn't.

Alex (*to Dinah*) Why would Tony want to attack *you*?

Dinah (*as if in a trance*) I don't know—you'd only just gone upstairs—I—I started to write a letter . . . you know, I told you . . . He sneaked in through the french windows . . . He was going to . . . (*She is unable to continue*)

Cathy goes to the buffet and pours a brandy

Alex Go on.

Dinah I—I thought he was the prowler you warned me about.

Alex Didn't you *know* it was Tony?

Dinah How could I have? I never knew him, or what he looked like. (*A pause*) God, what have I done?

Alex (*without any sympathy*) Your irrational fear of the unknown has really got you into one almighty mess this time.

Dinah (*reflecting*) Why did he creep in so mysteriously?

Alex He would have been expecting to find me and was probably just as surprised as you apparently were.

Cathy approaches them with the brandy

Dinah But—why did he sneak in through the french windows?

Cathy (*holding out the drink*) You've had a terrible and horrifying experience, drink this—it should help calm you.

Alex (*moving to take the drink*) Thank you.

Cathy (*handing the drink to Dinah*) It's for Dinah, you jerk.

Dinah (*taking the glass*) Thank you. (*She takes tentative sips of the brandy*) Why did he act so strangely?

There is a roll of thunder

Alex (*moving DC*) I don't know *what* you're talking about. Tony always comes in through the french windows if he's been working in the old barn. (*He clicks his fingers—something has just occurred to him*) God, I should have told you, it never occurred to me. I had the barn converted into a workshop where Tony does—(*corrects himself*)—did most of his research and experiments. It's quicker for him to come through the french windows than go round the cottage to the main door. He wouldn't have been expecting to find you here—I told him you were coming, but that you'd have left by early evening. As your car isn't in the yard he would have assumed— (*his grief stops him in midsentence. He inspects the plans again*) All this work . . . for nothing. (*He rolls up the plans and rests them against the side of the hi-fi*)

Dinah Why didn't he speak—say something?

Alex (*turning*) He's very shy with women. (*Moving past Tony's body*) I urged him to write to you but he wouldn't listen to me. I expect he'd be waiting for *you* to make the first move.

Cathy She certainly made the first move.

Alex (*to Cathy*) Fetch a sheet from the spare room, will you? We ought to cover the body.

Cathy exits to the spare room

(*Going to the desk*) I suppose I'd better phone the police and report the shooting.

Dinah (*rising to intercept Alex*) The *police*?

Alex Well there's damned little point in calling the fire brigade.

Dinah (*realising the reality of the situation*) But—I'd be arrested—charged with murder.

Cathy enters with a white bed sheet and drapes it over Tony's body. (Cathy should drape the sheet over the body in such a way that Dinah cannot see that the bloodstains are already there before *Cathy covers the body, but the audience can*)

Alex I would say that is a strong possibility.

Dinah I acted in self-defence—he *was* going to attack me. (*She looks pleadingly towards Cathy*) You saw him about to attack me, didn't you?

Cathy I'm sorry Dinah, but I can't testify to that. I'm sure you didn't mean to kill him but—well, all I saw was Tony lying there on the floor and you with the gun in your hand.

Dinah (*still pleading*) I'm *trying* to tell both of you what happened and neither of you will believe me. You could both say you saw him about to attack me, that you were unable to stop him and I had no alternative but to shoot him to protect myself.

Alex I'm sorry Dinah, but we can't testify to something we didn't see. Prosecuting Counsels have a sly way of trapping a witness once they've taken the stand and that would make us accessories to murder.

Dinah (*horror-struck*) Murder?

Alex (*in thought*) Tony was obviously coming to see me to discuss an idea he was working on and to show me the plans. That's no reason for you to have shot him. That's hardly likely to be a strong line of defence. (*Thinking*) No, you must tell the police that you thought he was an intruder out to steal the paintings, you caught him by surprise and he was going to attack you—it was either you or him, so you fired a warning shot but didn't mean to actually harm him. They *might* believe you—after all, there wasn't any motive, so you could get off with manslaughter.

Dinah (*reflecting*) I'd be sent to prison.

Alex A reduced sentence—with any luck you'd be out in ten years, less if you behaved well.

Cathy Prison? Dinah? They couldn't send Dinah to prison, surely? She's a national figure.

Alex I doubt if the law would take her reputation into account.

Cathy It's just that I can't imagine *Dinah* in prison—she's not a real criminal—not like those you see on the television. (*Remembering*) I saw a programme about a women's prison the other week—it was awful! Confined to a tiny cell, no privacy, squalid, most of them lesbians—

Alex Okay Cathy, right now I think Dinah has enough problems without your describing her room-mates. We'll have to try and get her a private cell.

Cathy I was just trying to be—

Alex All right Cathy, we realize you were only trying to be helpful. What say you leave Dinah and myself together for a while, and we'll try and sort out this whole terrible mess. I'll let you know when the police arrive, I imagine they'll want to take a statement from you.

Cathy Well—all right, if you think that's best.

Alex I think that's best.

Cathy (*moving towards the spare room; turning to Dinah*) I'm real sorry about all this, Dinah.

Cathy exits into the spare room, closing the door

Alex (*moving towards Tony's body; looking down*) God what a mess! All that blood! (*Turning to face Dinah*) There's only one thing for it.

Dinah (*hopefully*) Yes?

Alex I'll have to shampoo the carpet.

Dinah Don't you realize something terrible has happened?

Alex Of course I do.

They are both silent for a moment

Well, I guess I'd better call the police and report everything. (*He moves for the telephone*)

Dinah (*rising and intercepting him again*) Alex, no, please don't call them.

Alex What else do you expect me to do? There's been a homicide here.

Dinah (*moving near Tony's body*) You know they'd arrest me—it—it would be the end of everything for me. My career—think of my career. I'm the most popular columnist in Britain. The scandal would ruin me.

Alex (*a wry smile*) Yes, it certainly would!

Dinah All my fans would switch to Marje Proops. (*Or whoever is the 'number one' columnist of the day*)

Alex Dinah, I know how unfortunate the outcome is going to be for you, but I don't understand what you are trying to say. My partner lies on the lounge floor deceased, kaput, out of order, and the chief witness for the prosecution is in the spare room. The odds are hardly in your favour.

Dinah I realize that, but surely we can discuss this situation sensibly, rationally, and try to reach a satisfactory outcome.

Alex A satisfactory outcome? Who for?

Dinah remains silent. Alex knows what she is trying to say

We can't simply throw the body over the cliff and pretend nothing happened.

Dinah (*her composure recovered*) Why not?

Alex Why not? (*He hesitates*) These things just are not—I mean, it's simply not poss— (*He is tripping over his words*) You cannot be serious?

Dinah But I am Alex, I am very serious. (*She puts her glass on the desk*)

Alex I don't understand you at all.

There is another roll of thunder

Dinah (*indicating the body*) It was an unfortunate accident.

Alex Nobody knows that for certain.

Dinah Why *couldn't* you—I mean, why couldn't *we* dump the body? Over the cliff?

Alex Because it would be discovered by fishermen at low tide and when they see the bullet wound they'd know it wasn't a suicide leap.

Dinah (*definitely herself again*) Well then, we could chain the body to a block of concrete. The water is very deep near the cliff.

Alex (*clicking his fingers*) That's a great idea! I'll phone Readymix first thing and order the concrete.

Dinah You think that's funny? I don't think that's funny. We're in a desperate situation.

Alex (*enjoying the situation*) Correction. *You're* in a desperate situation.

Dinah Alex, you've got to help me. You *must* help me. If we can't throw the body over the cliff, you'll have to bury it on the cliff top—no-one goes near there, so it wouldn't be discovered.

Alex Not until some boy scouts pitch their tents there.

Dinah (*angrily*) Stop making futile excuses. Who else knows were Tony is tonight?

Alex How should I know?

Dinah His wife?

Alex He isn't—wasn't married.

Dinah Parents?

Alex They live abroad.

Dinah Girlfriend?

Alex (*a laugh*) Tony?

Dinah Any locals?

Alex He isn't too well known around these parts so I doubt anyone could prove that he was ... Just a moment, hang about, why am I answering these questions? Don't tell me I'm thinking the same as you. You're not *really* serious about this, are you?

Dinah Yes Alex, I am.

Alex (*incredulously*) You expect *me* to dump Tony's body over the cliff or bury it in some remote grave, just to please you—to get *you* out of an awkward corner? To pretend this dreadful incident never occurred?

Dinah (*desperately*) Please Alex, *darling*, you've got to help me.

Alex Why the hell should I, *darling*? If I was ever found out, I'd be as guilty as you—aiding and abetting a murderess, suppressing evidence. Give me *one* good reason why I should involve myself.

Dinah You're—my husband.

Alex Ex-hubby—

Dinah (*a pause*) I wouldn't expect you to do it for nothing.

Alex I don't follow.

Dinah I'd make it worth your while.

Alex (*mildly interested*) What exactly do you mean?

Dinah What is the one thing you want more than anything?

Alex (*thinking hard*) ... a "Dear Dinah" T-Shirt?

Dinah I mean financially.

Alex (*curious*) Go on.

Dinah I—would be prepared to re-negotiate the allowance—

Alex I'm listening.

Dinah . . . to half of what you pay me now.

Alex (*with a laugh*) That's hardly incentive enough—and I thought you needed the money so that you could redecorate your flat.

Dinah That will have to wait. (*She pauses*) Of course, I'd have my solicitor draw up a new agreement.

Alex (*moving towards the coffee table*) You'll have to do better than that, Dinah. (*He picks up his empty glass*)

Dinah State your price, then.

Alex considers his empty glass, and remains silent

Go on, answer me, what is your price?

Alex I'm thinking. I'm thinking.

Dinah (*after further consideration*) All right, a complete indemnity against any further payments to me.

Alex (*heading for the buffet*) You know, that's a very tempting offer.

Dinah That's all I *can* offer—that's all I have to bargain with.

Alex (*mixing a drink*) I have to ask myself, if I agreed, would it undermine my moral principles? I am after all, a man of integrity and honour. (*He sips his drink*) I have my duty to king and country. I have my obligations to the community. On the other hand—do you know . . . I'm almost embarrassed to say this, but I still find you a strikingly attractive woman. I know things didn't quite work out as we would have hoped, but it would be wrong of me to deny having any affection for you.

Dinah Cut the glossary Alex, are you going to help, or not?

Alex (*moving DC*) I suppose whatever happens now, nothing can bring Tony back. (*Looking down at the body*) I don't *really* want to see you charged with his murder. (*Turning to face Dinah*) Very well, I accept your offer.

Dinah (*relieved and moving towards Alex*) Alex, I can't begin to tell you what a weight off my mind that is.

Alex What are ex-husbands for if only to cover up the occasional indiscretion of one's former wife? (*He sips his drink*) There is one other consideration.

Dinah (*warily*) Yes?

Alex You quit starting every answer in your column with "I know exactly how you feel".

Dinah (*feeling it a considerable concession*) That is my trademark, do you absolutely insist I give *that* up?

Alex (*smiling*) I insist.

Dinah Oh, very well, seeing how you seem to have me at checkmate.

Alex (*finishes his drink in one victorious gulp*) Splendid. Well if we're going through with this, let's get started. By an unusual coincidence, I was digging near the cliff top only yesterday. We can bury the body there. (*He puts his empty glass on the coffee table*)

There is another roll of thunder as Alex goes to the french windows

Dinah Do you need any help from me?

Alex I think I'll be able to manage on my own. (*He pulls the curtains apart*) Ahhhh!

The cause of Alex's exclamation is a flash of lightning across the windows. Dinah shrieks simultaneously, in fright. Alex recovers

God, that flash of lightning nearly scared me to death! It's coming down like the monsoon out there, so *no way* am I playing at undertakers in that. I'll have to move the body in the morning.

Dinah (*moving to the rear of the sofa*) What, leave the body in here?

Alex (*moving towards Dinah*) He won't be going anywhere, will he?

Dinah I guess not, Christ now I'm saying it. (*Pause*) What will you tell Cathy? I don't think she is going to be *too* happy about what we have arranged.

Alex (*loosening his tie and the top button of his shirt*) Don't worry about Cathy, I'll take care of her. She won't cause any trouble.

Dinah Are you sure about that?

Alex Absolutely. (*A pause*) There's nothing more we can do until the morning, so let's call it a day and turn in. (*He switches off the standard lamp then goes to the desk*)

Dinah Yes, I'd almost forgotten how tired I was. (*Moving to the staircase*) Alex?

Alex (*at the desk, turning*) Yes?

Dinah I don't know what I can say, other than "thank you".

Alex (*switching off the desk lamp*) I wish I could say "the pleasure's mine"—but I can't. (*He moves to the staircase*)

Dinah climbs the staircase, stops, turns and looks DC

Dinah I don't suppose I'll realize the sheer horror of what has happened until the morning. I really am very sorry about Tony.

Alex We are all deeply shocked by what has happened. (*He follows Dinah up the staircase*)

Dinah It's such an horrific and tragic end for him. So sudden. One minute alive and the next ... He had his whole life ahead of him, but nothing has gone according to plan for him, has it?

Alex (*turning to look in the direction of the body*) No ... I don't suppose it has ...

Thunder rolls and forked lightning flashes across the sky, giving eerie illumination to the room as—

the CURTAIN *falls*

ACT II

SCENE 1

The same. Early Saturday morning

When the Curtain rises, the lounge is unoccupied. The french windows are open to bright sunshine. The bloodstained bedsheet is lying in a crumpled heap in front of the sofa, and the door to the spare room is partly open. Alex enters through the french windows, closing them behind him. He is wearing old slacks and a sweater, probably because he has had dirty work to do—burying Tony's body for instance. He glances around the room, goes to the spare room and looks in, then closes the door; he is clearly puzzled about something. He comes DC as Dinah descends the staircase. She is wearing a dressing gown over a pair of Alex's pyjamas

Dinah (*scanning the room*) You've moved the body?

Alex (*lifting the bedsheet with one hand, feeling beneath it with the other in mocking sarcasm*) My God! It's gone! What have you done with it?

Dinah (*moving DC*) I was trying to ask a serious question. Where have you moved the body?

Alex It's propped up in the shower cubicle.

Dinah Alex, it's a little early in the morning for your gags. Are you going to tell me where it is?

Alex It's safe.

Dinah You're sure it won't be found?

Alex Not for at least fifty years, by which time we'll both have joined him, unless someone has discovered the secret of immortality. The less you know, the better.

Dinah How gallant you are.

Alex I wish you would appear a little more appreciative, I've only done all this to help you out of one hell of an awkward spot. My entire reputation is on the line.

Dinah Oh, I thought *your* interest was solely financial.

Alex Why am I so misjudged by everyone?

Dinah You're not. You must have been up early if you've moved the body already. Couldn't you sleep?

Alex Quite the contrary, I slept soundly—I didn't wake up 'till half six. How about you?

Dinah How would you expect after last night? I hardly slept at all, tossed and turned all night. I find it hard to believe you had an undisturbed night.

Alex Well I did. Once my head hit the pillow, I was away.

Dinah (*puzzled*) Really? Then what was all the commotion?

Alex (*equally puzzled*) Commotion? What commotion?

Dinah During the night. I don't know what time it would have been—the bedside clock had stopped, but I heard raised voices, and what I thought was a scream, then it went quiet. Later, I heard a car drive away. What was going on?

Alex I have no idea, I told you, I slept like a log—woke up in the fireplace. (*He raises a hand in defence*) Sorry, no gags this morning. Why didn't *you* come down to investigate?

Dinah After what happened last night? No fear. I kept my door firmly locked—you wouldn't have got me down here, not with a corpse lying in the room.

Alex You were probably dreaming another of your X-certificate nightmares.

Dinah It was *too* realistic for it to have been a dream. What are you trying to cover up—a row with Cathy?

Alex I'm not trying to cover up anything.

Dinah Then where *is* Picasso this morning?

Alex (*hesitating*) I don't know. Her bed doesn't look as though it's been slept in and her van isn't in the yard.

Dinah I knew we couldn't trust her.

Alex What is that supposed to mean?

Dinah (*clearly delighted*) Isn't it obvious? She's walked out on you!

Alex Don't be ridiculous . . . she's in love with me!

Dinah God, how vulnerable men are! (*A lecture*) She is in love with your money and your possessions—not you. She'll tag along with you for a while—until you stop subsidizing her paintings, then when she meets some tall, blue-eyed, blond-haired playboy with a bronzed body, she'll be up and away and all *you'll* have will be fond memories and a feeling of bitterness. I deal with problems like this every day—my mail is full of them, and I always have to give the same advice—don't have delusions of grandeur because you'll end up very, very disappointed.

Alex I wish I'd written to you earlier!

Dinah You ought to take notice of what I've just told you—I can help you if you'll listen.

Alex Mind if I take a second opinion from Marje Proops?

Dinah (*bitterly*) I wish you hadn't mentioned *her*.

Alex How long it takes for the wounds to heal.

Dinah I suppose it was you and Cathy I heard quarrelling last night. Now that she knows about our—arrangement—we'll probably find ourselves the victims of her blackmail demands.

Alex That's nonsense, Cathy would never . . . anyway, I haven't even had the chance to talk with her about our—unethical compromise.

Dinah The absence of the police must have alerted her to something.

Alex She probably thought it best to return to the studio until everything has blown over. It's better for us if she doesn't get involved.

Dinah A fine witness she'd be, fleeing the scene of the crime—sorry, I should have said incident.

Alex If it will make you feel any easier, I'll phone her and find out what she is up to. (*He goes to the desk, lifts up the telephone receiver, and is about to dial*)

There is a loud knocking at the door

Who can that be? (*He replaces the receiver*)

Dinah Your social worker?

Alex I thought we agreed—no gags. It can't be Cathy because she has her own key, and I didn't hear her van pull up, did you?

Dinah No, I don't think so.

Loud knocking is again heard

Alex I'll see who it is. (*He goes to exit, stops, turns quickly*) The bedsheet—hide it. Quickly.

Dinah reluctantly picks up the bedsheet, starts to stuff it behind a cushion on the sofa, but realizes it will not be totally concealed

The cupboard—throw it in one of the cupboards.

Dinah takes the sheet to the large understairs cupboard, and as she opens the door, a broom falls out against her, causing her to gasp. She pushes the broom back inside, throws in the bedsheet and closes the door

Relieved, Alex goes to answer the door

(*Off*) Yes?

Weaver (*off*) Mr Conrad?

Alex (*off*) Yes.

Weaver (*off*) Mr *Alex* Conrad?

Alex (*off*) That is correct.

Weaver (*off*) Detective Inspector Weaver, C.I.D. Excuse me calling so early, but I wonder if I might have a few words with you. May I come in?

Alex (*off*) Er—yes, of course.

Alex follows Weaver into the room. He seems an unpleasant, humourless sort of man, late forties, and is wearing a grey, well-worn gabardine raincoat and trilby hat, His shoes are slightly muddy. On noticing Dinah, he removes his hat, inviting Alex to make the introductions

My wife, or I should say, my estranged wife, Dinah. Dinah this is Detective Inspector—

Weaver Weaver. (*A brief nod to Dinah*) Mrs Conrad. (*He puts his hat on the sofa*) I've already apologized to Mr Conrad for calling so early, but— Dinah Conrad? You wouldn't by any chance be *the* Dinah Conrad? The columnist?

Dinah I'm afraid so.

Weaver (*moving forward to shake her hand firmly*) No kidding! Well how about that! My wife reads your column every week—never misses it!

Dinah I'm flattered.

Weaver (*releasing her hand*) Keeps threatening to leave me! You know how it is—a policeman's work is never done. The unsocial hours, never at home to give 'Lizbeth and the kids the love and devotion they need.

Dinah and Weaver move DC

Dinah I know exactly how you feel. The symptoms are not uncommon, and of course, working all those irregular hours is bound to put a strain on *any* marriage. I can give you the address of an organization you could contact—they will be able to give you help and guidance.

Weaver I must say, that's very considerate of you, Mrs Conrad.

Alex looks on helplessly

Dinah Not at all, Inspector, not at all. How many children do you have?

Weaver Two. Susie is nine and Nigel eight, well—not quite eight—he will be in a couple of months. I have some photos—would you like to see them? (*He reaches into his inside pocket*)

Dinah I'd love to.

Alex (*impatiently*) Inspector, I don't wish to appear rude, but you did say you wanted a few words with me about something.

Weaver (*deciding not to bother with the photographs after all*) Yes, of course, do forgive me for digressing. Actually, this is only a routine call to check that everything is all right.

Alex What do you mean—to check everything is all right? Everything is fine.

Weaver Well, was there—any trouble here last night?

Alex Trouble, Inspector?

Weaver A disturbance, then?

Alex No, I don't think so. Dinah and I had an argument about who should wipe the dishes, but other than that—what makes you think—

Weaver Just a report we had. Young couple thought they heard a gunshot.

Dinah (*feigning surprise*) A gunshot, Inspector?

Weaver That is what was reported, madam. Couple of tourists—stopped near here to check directions—or something—they thought they heard a gunshot.

Alex About what time would this have been?

Weaver takes a notebook from his pocket and consults it

Weaver About ten o'clock as near as they can recall.

Alex Well, you certainly took your time getting here. Dinah and I could have been badly—

Weaver The matter wasn't reported until this morning, sir. They checked into the hotel in the village for the night, and didn't go out again because of the storm. They called in at the station before setting off again and I came as quickly as I could.

Alex We appreciate your calling, Inspector, but as you can see, there wasn't any trouble here and everything is in apple-pie order. Perhaps your informants heard a car backfire.

Weaver They were certain it was a gunshot, sir—(*he checks his notebook again*)—and you *did* report a prowler in the area the other week. (*He puts his notebook away*)

Alex Yes, well, if there *had* been any serious trouble here last night, I'd have contacted you immediately.

Weaver I'm sure you would have, sir. (*He checks his watch*) Sorry to have taken up so much of your time unnecessarily. (*He collects his hat*) Next case—stolen car radios . . . There's an exciting day for you.

The telephone rings

Dinah (*to Weaver*) I'll see you out, Inspector.

Dinah is showing Weaver to the door as Alex answers the telephone

Alex Two-two-four-six-five ... Yes, this is Mr Conrad speaking ... Yes, he is—just a moment. (*He covers the receiver with one hand and calls out to Weaver*) Oh, Inspector, it's for you.

Weaver turns and goes to the desk. Dinah stops by the side of the sofa

Weaver (*taking the receiver from Alex*) Thank you.

Alex slowly goes DC giving Dinah a puzzled glance

Weaver ... no, I was just leaving—seems to have been a false alarm ... Who? ... She's here with her husband right now, or rather, her *estranged* husband ... What? ... Good God! I'd better get all this down. (*He takes his notebook from his pocket and starts taking notes using Dinah's pen*) Give me that again ... hold on, hold on, not so fast, I don't do Pitman's shorthand ... yes ... yes ... you don't say? And I thought I was in for a quiet day ...

Alex and Dinah look at each other apprehensively

... Any idea of the time? ... Yes, yes, I appreciate that ... still looking for it? ... Identification? ... Is that e.r. or a.r.? ... And the name of that place again? ... No, I can spell it ... I'll say, right out of Bulldog Drummond. I thought I was going to be chasing stolen car radios all day ... Okay, I've got most of that. I'll handle things at this end and join you later. Who's there from the local boys? ...

Alex and Dinah are now extremely concerned. Dinah moves nearer to Alex, Weaver puts Dinah's pen down

... Tindle? Just my luck—our paths have crossed once before. Do me one favour will you? Have someone call my wife and tell her not to wait up ... Yes, fifth time this week. She'll probably file for divorce first thing Monday morning ... Good-bye. (*He slowly puts the receiver down*)
Alex (*unable to hide his anxiety*) Is anything wrong, Inspector?

Weaver ignores the question and puts his hat on the sofa, then goes over to the bookcase, consulting his notebook

Weaver (*turning*) Do you still insist there wasn't any trouble here last night?
Dinah We've told you there wasn't, Inspector. Isn't that enough to satisfy you? Alex said he would have reported any.

Weaver starts to look over Alex's collection of books. Alex starts to move nearer to Weaver, and Dinah goes to the front of the sofa

Weaver (*turning*) You have an admirable collection of detective novels, Mr Conrad.
Alex (*proudly*) It is renowned as one of the finest collections of its kind in the country. I give lectures—

Weaver Lectures?

Alex Well, talks. Women's Institute, that sort of thing.

Weaver (*passing along the bookshelves checking the titles*) Personally, I disapprove of this type of literature—amateur detectives and snoopy old ladies uncovering vital clues overlooked by the police and thus revealing the identity of the murderer. (*He turns to Dinah*) Or murderess. Makes us out to be inept and foolish. (*He moves DC*) I can assure you both that I am anything but inept and foolish.

Alex They're only fiction, Inspector. I wouldn't begin to underestimate your ability. I'm sure you do a magnificent job under very difficult conditions.

Weaver And people like *you* don't make it any easier.

Dinah *What* is that supposed to mean, Inspector?

Weaver (*after a pause*) That telephone call was from headquarters. I regret I must ask you some more questions Mrs Conrad, Mr Conrad.

Alex Fire away.

Weaver I beg your pardon?

Alex (*taken aback*) A figure of speech.

Weaver Most inappropriate in the circumstances. (*He consults his notebook then turns to Dinah*) Mrs Conrad, do you reside at three-hundred and forty-two Harlington Gardens?

Dinah (*puzzled*) Yes, that's my address.

Weaver Where were you last night?

Dinah I was—here.

Weaver (*surprised*) Here? What time did you return home?

Dinah I didn't—I stayed here the whole night.

Weaver The *whole* night?

Dinah (*angry*) That is what I said, Inspector.

Weaver (*to Alex*) I thought you said *estranged* wife, sir?

Alex Yes, I did.

Weaver (*suavely*) I see.

Dinah I came here yesterday evening to discuss some matters which frankly don't concern you. My car broke down on the way and won't be ready until later today, so I had to stay here overnight—hence my wearing my husband's pyjamas.

Weaver (*to Alex*) Can you verify that, sir?

Alex Yes Inspector, those are definitely my pyjamas.

Weaver (*not amused*) I mean about Mrs Conrad being here *all* night.

Alex We didn't sleep together, if that is what you are suggesting.

Weaver That is not what I am suggesting—I have no interest in your nocturnal habits whatsoever.

Alex We both retired at about the same time.

Weaver Which was?

Alex I don't remember exactly—ten, eleven.

Weaver Did you see your wife to her room?

Alex She knows where it is.

Weaver Very droll, sir. Tell me, are you a light sleeper?

Alex I usually sleep quite soundly... Inspector, what is the purpose of all these questions?

Weaver (*continuing*) So Mrs Conrad could have left her room, gone out, returned, and you might not have known?

Dinah starts to move nearer Weaver in protest

Alex Well—yes—I suppose she could have.

Dinah (*to Weaver*) Inspector, where is all this leading?—

Weaver (*to Alex, cutting her off*) I take it then that you cannot vouch for your wife's whereabouts last night after you both retired. You can't *swear* as to where she might, or might not have been?

Alex (*resignedly*) No, I can't.

Dinah (*impatiently*) Will you *please* come to the point, Inspector.

Weaver In good time, madam. (*To Alex*) Mr Conrad, I believe you own a gun?

Alex Er—yes, I do.

Weaver May I see it please?

Alex Yes, of course. (*He goes to the desk, opens the top right-hand drawer and rummages about in it*) Strange, I keep it in this drawer, but it appears to be missing.

Weaver (*concerned*) Missing?

Alex (*checking in the other drawers*) I don't know where it could be. (*To Dinah*) Have *you* moved it, Dinah?

Dinah (*firmly*) I didn't even know you kept a gun.

Weaver (*to Alex*) When did you last see your gun?

Alex (*after closing the drawer*) I don't know for certain. I cleaned it a couple of weeks ago.

Weaver You keep the drawer locked?

Alex (*hesitating*) . . . No.

Weaver (*incredulously*) No? . . . why ever not?

Alex Well—if I needed to use it quickly—

Weaver Lot of gangsters around these parts, are there?

Alex (*after a slight pause*) I have a valuable collection of books and paintings. If word got out—

Weaver I understand, sir. So—anyone could have taken the gun without your knowing?

Alex (*with slight relief*) Yes—I suppose they could have.

Weaver You ought to keep your gun in a safer place sir, so no-one has easy access to it.

Alex I'll be sure and find a safer place, once I've found it . . . Inspector, would you please come to the point of this interrogation?

Weaver Very well. (*He consults his notebook*) Did either of you know a—Tony Westerby?

Dinah shakes her head to say 'no'

Alex He is my business partner—Inspector, what do you mean—*did* we know him?

Weaver I'm very sorry to have to tell you that he's dead.

Alex Dead? (*He is visibly shocked*) Tony? My God . . . Do you know who shot him?

Weaver Who said anything about him being shot?

Alex I—assumed with your asking about the gun—what happened then? Has he been involved in a car accident?

Weaver No sir, he's been shot. Twice. Two bullet wounds, one of them fatal.

Dinah *Two* bullet wounds?

Weaver That is my information.

Alex I—I don't know what to say. Tony? (*Clearly shaken*) Who would want to murder Tony?

Weaver Who mentioned anything about murder?

Alex I assumed—you mean—he shot himself? Suicide?

Weaver No sir, he was murdered. Suicides don't usually shoot themselves twice, do they?

Alex No—no, of course not. How stupid of me to suggest that.

Weaver If it *had* been suicide, we would have found the gun near his body, but we haven't been able to find it yet.

Alex Haven't been able to find the body?

Weaver (*again not amused*) Haven't been able to find the *gun.* I understand he was shot from close range and that one of the bullets passed clean through his body. They're searching for that bullet now—as well as the murder weapon. That's why I'm anxious to check your gun—to eliminate it from our enquiries of course. When we've found the gun and the bullet, our ballistics people will be able to match them. (*A pause, then to Dinah*) Now, Mrs Conrad, how long had you known Mr Westerby?

Dinah I told you—I didn't know him at all.

Weaver (*surprised*) What?

Dinah Alex and I have been separated for over three years so I know very little about his activities, let alone his business associates.

Weaver Then may I suggest that you knew him under a different name?

Dinah What makes you think that I knew him at all?

Weaver . . . His body was found in *your* flat.

Dinah (*collapsing on to the sofa*) In *my* flat—that—that's impossible.

Weaver Is it madam?

Dinah Inspector, I can assure you that I didn't know my husband's partner under either his own name or any other.

Weaver It certainly seems he knew you.

Alex What are you suggesting, Inspector? Dinah did not know my late partner at all.

Weaver (*to Alex*) What I *do* know is that Mr Westerby's body was found in your wife's flat. Apparently there are no signs of a forced entry *or* evidence of a struggle, so it would appear your partner had been—invited in.

Dinah (*rising*) This is absurd.

Weaver (*continuing*) To keep an appointment, as a matter of fact.

Dinah What on earth are you talking about? I was here *all* night.

Weaver (*to Dinah*) It appears that Mr Westerby was keeping an appointment with *you.* We've found a book of matches in one of his pockets—you know— the type they give you in clubs and restaurants, and on the back of it had been scribbled *your* telephone number, yesterday's date and a time—(*He checks his notes*)—eleven-thirty. We don't know if that's eleven-thirty in the morning or at night, but since they estimate the time of death as between eleven p.m. and two a.m., it would seem that the deceased called on you last night. Probably went straight to your flat from the restaurant—the— (*another check of his notes*)—"Green Pagoda". Do you know that restaurant, Mrs Conrad?

Dinah ⎤ (*together*)   Never heard of it.
Alex ⎦   Isn't that the restaurant where Hetty saw you?

Dinah (*angrily*) Thank you very much.

Weaver Ah! Now we have a difference of opinion, a clash of alibis! (*To Dinah*) Mrs Conrad, I am far from satisfied with your explanations, or rather, the lack of them, and in the circumstances I must formally caution you that you are not obliged to say anything unless you wish to do so, but that what you do say may be put into writing and given in evidence.

Dinah This is outrageous! (*To Alex*) Alex, are you going to let the Inspector speak to me like that?

Alex (*to Weaver*) Yes, I say, Inspector, isn't this all a bit heavy-handed? Do you intend to charge my wife with murder?

Weaver I'm not charging anyone . . . yet.

Alex (*to Dinah*) Dinah, I don't think you ought to answer any further questions until you have consulted with your solicitor.

Weaver (*to Dinah*) Mrs Conrad, it is your right to take the advice of your solicitor, if you wish to do so, but I think we can get to the bottom of this if you will just answer a few more questions.

Dinah Go ahead, I have nothing to hide.

Alex Dinah, I think you're making a big mistake.

Dinah Let the Inspector continue.

Weaver (*to Alex*) When did you last see Mr Westerby *alive*?

Alex Yesterday afternoon—and I take it your tone implies that I also saw him dead?

Weaver Did you?

Alex (*after a pause*) Certainly not.

Weaver (*pacing the room*) This is a most intriguing situation. You can't account for your wife's whereabouts last night, your wife denies ever having known the deceased, yet he turns up at her flat to keep an appointment and is shot twice: Your gun is mysteriously missing and your wife's car inconveniently— or *conveniently* broken down. On top of all that, I come out here following a report that someone heard a gunshot . . . I'm afraid your story is like a Swiss cheese.

Dinah A Swiss cheese?

Weaver Full of holes. (*He beams at having cracked a howler*)

Neither Alex or Dinah appreciate the joke

Alex Oh—very good Inspector, I must remember that one for the golf club. As a point of interest who *conveniently* discovered the body?

Weaver That I don't know. I only took down the essential details. Perhaps your wife can throw some light on who could have discovered the body. (*He looks sternly at Dinah*)

Dinah It was probably Gertie—my cleaning lady. She does three mornings a week including Saturdays.

Alex (*a thought*) Maybe *Gertie* shot him—perhaps his apppointment was with *her*. (*To Dinah*) Could *they* have been having an affair?

Dinah (*shaking her head*) Gertie is sixty-three.

Weaver There's *one* theory discounted. (*He checks his notebook then snaps it shut*) I think that's all for the moment. I trust neither of you will be leaving here for a while? (*He puts his notebook in his pocket*)

Alex I wasn't going to abscond.

Dinah I'm going back to my flat as soon as my car is ready.

Weaver You can't—not yet—not until the forensic people and the photographer are through. I'll let you know when you can return but meanwhile, I suggest you stay here, if your *estranged* husband will accommodate you. (*He collects his hat and turns to Alex*) You *will* make a thorough search for your gun and let me know immediately you have found it?

Alex Of course, Inspector—I'll turn the house upside down.

Weaver (*heading for the exit*) I'm going to your wife's flat now, so you can contact me there if necessary. Oh, one other thing, where can I contact Mr Westerby's next of kin? I'll need to inform them of this—unfortunate situation.

Alex Tony wasn't married and his parents live abroad—I'm not exactly sure where.

Weaver In that case, it may be necessary for you to make a formal identification of the body—I'll let you know.

Alex I understand, Inspector.

Weaver (*putting on his hat*) Some day *this* is going to be. I come here on a routine call and find myself in a full-scale murder investigation. I suppose it's better than chasing after stolen car radios though. (*A pause*) I'll see myself out—good day Mr Conrad—Mrs Conrad. (*He is about to exit but stops and turns to Dinah*) And Mrs Conrad.

Dinah (*startled*) Yes?

Weaver You *will* let me have the address of that organization you mentioned?

Dinah (*relieved*) Oh—yes, of course.

Alex shows Weaver to the main door and returns

Dinah is unable to conceal her rage and anger

You bastard!

Alex (*stuttering*) I—I—I—

Dinah You dirty double-crossing sonofabitch.

Alex I—I—I—

Dinah You conniving shyster!

Alex I—I—I—

Dinah Oh, for God's sake stop stuttering and say something positive.

Alex I—I— (*he turns to the buffet*) I need a drink.

Dinah How bloody typical of you.

Alex, his hand shaking, unsteadily pours a drink. Dinah looks on in disgust

That's right—retreat into your whisky decanter like a trapped water rat!

Alex takes an unsteady swig of his drink

Is *this* your idea of a deal? Your demonstration of a bargain?

Alex (*moving nearer Dinah*) Dinah, I swear I know nothing about all this, I'm as shocked and surprised as you are. (*He takes another shaky swig of his drink*)

Dinah Planting everything on me like that.

Alex I swear—

Dinah You swear a lot, don't you? What was that fairy story you told me just before the Inspector arrived? About having disposed of the body?

Alex I—I—

Dinah (*unrelenting*) Don't start that again.

Alex (*in desperate explanation*) I came down, discovered the body was missing —then I noticed Cathy's van wasn't in the yard. I *had* to make up the story on the spur of the moment.

Dinah Of course there isn't any sign of the body, because it's in *my* flat and that Inspector seems to think I shot him.

Alex You did—

Dinah But not *twice*. The Inspector said he'd been shot twice. (*Thinking*) Alex, it is now perfectly clear to me that you and Cathy have double-crossed me.

Alex (*incredulously*) What?

Dinah You have both set me up.

Alex That's ludicrous.

Dinah (*slowly pacing the room in thought*) Maybe Tony *wasn't* dead when I shot him—unconscious yes, but *not* dead. With Cathy's help, you carried him to her van—that would explain all the commotion I heard—then you drove to my flat, dumped the body there and came back.

Alex That really is an unlikely sequence of events, and if it were true, where's Cathy?

Dinah She probably drove you back here then went on to her studio. You said her van isn't in the yard.

Alex What about the other shot? If I'd shot him in your flat, your neighbours would have heard.

Dinah (*a little excited at figuring everything out*) You discovered he wasn't dead *before* you reached my flat, so you pulled into a country lane somewhere and—finished him off.

Alex And how did I get into your flat? I don't have a key and it's hardly likely I'd have been able to climb the drainpipe with an inert body over my shoulders.

Dinah (*checking her bag*) My keys are missing.

Alex Didn't you leave them at the garage? Your car keys would be on the same ring, wouldn't they?

Dinah (*pausing for thought*) I took the car keys off before giving them to the mechanic—in case you agreed to drive me home—I wouldn't have been able to get in.

Alex Well, I don't have your keys.

Dinah All right, if that's the way you want to play it.

Alex Look—I'll 'phone Cathy right now—you can speak with her yourself and she'll confirm your accusations are unfounded. (*He puts his glass on the coffee table*)

Dinah Of course she will, since she is just as involved as you.

Alex Hmm ... I'd like to know where Cathy is. (*He goes to the telephone and dials Cathy's number*) I'd *also* like to know how the police got on to us so quickly ... (*Holding the receiver away*) That's odd, there's no answer. (*He replaces the receiver*)

Dinah It was probably Cathy who alerted the police.

Alex Why would she do that?

Dinah A preliminary instalment to frighten us, turn us into a state of panic. The blackmail demands come next.

Alex I can't believe that.

Dinah You mean you don't *want* to believe it. (*Pauses*) What did that Inspector say about one of the bullets?

Alex Passed straight through the body?

Dinah That's right. (*Mighty relieved*) That's *me* off the hook, then.

Alex What do you mean?

Dinah I mean—I couldn't have killed Tony—could I? It's obvious the shot I fired went straight through him—otherwise it wouldn't have been necessary for you or Cathy to have shot him again—would it?

Alex (*thinking hard*) If you *did* fire the bullet that passed through him, it must be in this room somewhere—either lodged in the furniture or the wall. We'd better find it before the police do.

Dinah *You* told me he was dead after I'd shot him—

Alex I *thought* he was dead—it certainly appeared he was. You fired from point blank range and he was bleeding heavily, but he may simply have passed out. Right now, I think we had better concentrate on finding the bullet. It *must* be here somewhere. We'll have to re-enact the shooting.

Dinah The shooting? (*Shrugging*) Why?

Alex For God's sake Dinah, so that we can calculate the trajectory of the bullet. I'll be Tony—can you remember exactly where he was when you fired the shot.

Dinah Well, I think—near, near this side of the sofa. (*She points vaguely to the place*)

Alex Where were *you* when you shot him?

Dinah (*moving to the desk*) Here.

Alex Okay, now pretend that you have the gun in your hand and aim at me.

Dinah does as instructed, Alex co-ordinates

So if the bullet passed through his shoulder, it would have hit ... (*He turns to face L*)

Dinah The far wall.

Alex (*moving towards the hi-fi*) I hope it hasn't damaged anything. (*He checks the wall area*) Can't seem to find anything. (*He searches harder*) Could be it wasn't that shot after all.

Dinah It was worth a try.

Alex (*still searching*) It would have put us one up on the police. We'll just
   have to—wait, what's this?

Dinah (*excitedly*) Have you found it?

Alex (*removing the bullet from the painting*) It was stuck in Cathy's painting.
   (*He turns to face Dinah*)

Dinah (*moving towards Alex*) You're very lucky.

Alex What do you mean?

Dinah It only damaged the painting—it could have ruined the frame.

Alex Very amusing. (*He shows the bullet to Dinah*) Look—there's a tiny smear
   of blood on it.

Dinah takes the bullet and inspects it

   That *has* to be the bullet Weaver was on about.

Dinah puts the bullet in her dressing gown pocket

   Good job he didn't start looking for clues when he was here. Clever, though,
   how he knew about my gun, obviously did his homework on me—a rather
   shrewd detective.

Dinah Not as shrewd as you think.

Alex No?

Dinah He didn't notice the bloodstains on the carpet, did he?

Alex Christ, the bloodstains! I'd almost forgotten about them, we'd better clean
   the carpet in case he comes back.

Dinah Yes, hadn't we just. Get some cleaning things will you? I'll need a
   bucket, brush, some powder—

Alex (*dashing for the kitchen*) I'll get a bucket and powder from the kitchen—
   there's a brush in the cupboard. (*He indicates the small cupboard under
   the stairs*)

Alex exits

*Dinah opens the cupboard and immediately lets out a scream, the cause of
which is Cathy's body falling out. She has been strangled—Alex's club tie
around her neck, and clutched in her hand is the handkerchief from the breast
pocket of Alex's jacket*

   Alex races back into the room, sees Cathy's body and stops, horrified

   Cathy! Oh my God! Cathy! (*He kneels down and lifts Cathy's inert head*)

Dinah (*rising, moving away*) Murderer!

Alex (*turning*) What?

Dinah You murderer!

Alex (*gently releasing Cathy's head and rising*) Why are you accusing me?

Dinah (*backing away*) First Tony, then Cathy.

Alex (*moving after Dinah*) You don't believe *I'm* responsible?

Dinah (*moving slowly DC*) Why? (*She turns to face Alex*) Why did you do
   it?

Alex *You* shot Tony. I—don't know anything about Cathy's murder. I didn't
   kill her, I swear I didn't.

Dinah (*moving back nearer the body*) The tie—the tie she's been strangled
   with—it's your club tie and you were wearing it last night.

Alex (*also moving back to the body*) There must be others like it.

Dinah The handkerchief—in her hand—it's the one you had in your breast pocket. (*She moves slowly to the front of the sofa*) That poor girl—she must have grabbed at the handkerchief and pulled it from your pocket as you strangled her. *Now* I know what you meant when you said she wouldn't cause any trouble and that you would take care of her.

Alex (*moving after Dinah*) You know I was speaking metaphorically.

Dinah (*moving away from Alex*) Stay away from me, you maniac.

Alex I didn't strangle her—it's obvious I've been set up!

Dinah Alex, really.

Alex (*almost pleading*) If *I'd* killed her, do you think I'd have left my calling card? And what reason had I to kill her? More's the motive I'd have to kill *you*!

Loud knocking at the door startles them both

Christ, who's that? (*Thinking*) Quick, help me push Cathy's body back in the cupboard.

Dinah (*horrified*) What?

Alex I'll have to answer the door, so for God's sake help me with the body.

Dinah, reduced to whimpering sobs, helps Alex with the body. Not without some difficulty, they manage to get it back into the cupboard. As Alex pushes the cupboard door closed, the door knocker sounds again

Alex pulls himself together and goes to answer the door

(*Off*) Inspector!

Weaver (*off*) Mr Conrad.

Weaver enters the room, followed by Alex

Mrs Conrad.

Dinah (*almost breathless*) Hello again, Inspector.

Weaver Sorry to impose on you a second time, but there was *one* other question I overlooked.

Alex What's that, Inspector?

Weaver Do you know there's a van blocking the entrance to your lane?

Alex A van?

Weaver Bit of an old banger. Has—(*He checks his notebook*) "Vanagio Studios" in faded lettering on the side. (*He puts his notebook away*) Know anything about it?

Alex No—I don't. It's probably been abandoned by someone, amazing where people leave their scrap metal these days.

Weaver Yes, unless it broke down in last night's storm. As it's blocking your lane, I couldn't get the squad car up. Almost ruined my shoes trudging through all that mud. (*A pause*) I'd arrange to have that van towed away, if I were you, sir.

Alex Yes, I'll attend to that straight away.

Weaver Well, I think that definitely is all this time, thank you. Good day, Mrs Conrad.

Dinah nods a silent farewell, but as Weaver turns to leave, followed by Alex, the understairs cupboard door slowly opens and Cathy's body starts to fall out. Dinah is able to push the door closed before Weaver notices anything, but Alex, having seen what happened, is having kittens

Mr Conrad, are you feeling all right? You've turned quite pale. (*A slight pause*) Not hiding a skeleton in the cupboard, are you? (*He laughs at his own droll joke*)

Alex (*forcing a laugh*) Inspector—the very thought . . .

The lights fade to—

Black-out

SCENE 2

The same. Only a few seconds have elapsed

Dinah is showing obvious relief and Alex returns, having seen Weaver to the door

Alex God, that was a close one. If Weaver had seen Cathy's body, that would have been it—an open-and-shut case.

Dinah (*coming DC*) Alex, if that was meant as a pun, it was in distinctly bad taste.

Alex Pun? Oh, you mean the cupboard door—open-and-shut. No, I didn't mean it as a joke—I don't feel much like joking right now. I meant, we only just got rid of Weaver in time. (*He moves nearer to Dinah*)

Dinah Never mind about Weaver, *you'd* better start trying to convince me that you didn't murder them both.

Alex I've already told you—if I had, do you think I'd have left such damaging evidence?

Dinah (*hesitating*) I don't know . . . I just don't know. You are cunning and devious and something tells me you are trying an elaborate double-bluff.

Alex How so?

Dinah By making it appear so obvious you did it, the police will think you've been—set up, as you described it. A very clever bluff.

Alex I'm not *that* devious—it's perfectly clear I *have* been set up. (*Rubbing his chin*) Someone, somewhere doesn't like me.

Dinah *Darling*, whatever makes you think that? You're such a warm-hearted, adorable old—

Alex You through with the character reference?

Dinah You're trying an elaborate double-bluff, but it won't work with me.

Alex You haven't answered *why* I killed Cathy, what can I gain? There's a notable absence of motive.

Dinah Not so. Perhaps you thought her paintings would be worth more if she was dead.

Alex You didn't seem to think they were worth much last night.

Dinah I may have—misjudged the girl.

Alex What? "Dear Dinah" making an error of judgement? Not what your readers would expect of you, is it? (*Almost as an afterthought*) And another thing—why would I hide her body in the cupboard?

Dinah All part of your bluff. (*Moving towards the large understairs cupboard*) Do you still insist that you didn't leave the cottage last night? (*She opens the cupboard door*)

Alex I told you—I slept like a log.

Dinah (*taking a pair of shoes out of the cupboard*) Then *how* do you explain these? (*She holds the shoes for Alex to see*)

Alex (*hesitating*) Bought them at Harrods—fifteen quid off in the sale.

Dinah You *know* what I mean, wise guy. They're covered in mud—(*touching the soles*)—and it's still quite soft.

Alex How did you *know* those shoes were in the cupboard?

Dinah I noticed them when I threw the bedsheet in. I didn't realize their significance until Weaver said Cathy's van was blocking the lane. (*She puts the shoes back in the cupboard and closes the door*)

Alex Significance? What are you trying to say?

Dinah (*turning*) You *had* to leave Cathy's van at the bottom of the lane because of the storm—it left the lane too muddy for you to drive up, so you walked back, hence the fresh mud on your shoes.

Alex (*desperately*) *Someone has set me up!*

Dinah Oh, don't be so pathetic. No-one has set you up. There *is* only one explanation. You decided to plant Tony's body in the flat. When you discovered he wasn't dead, you shot him again. You took the body in Cathy's van, which you had to leave at the bottom of the lane, and walked back. When you told Cathy what you'd done, she wouldn't go along with the idea, and threatened to notify the police, so you had to silence her. (*She pauses*) *That* would account for the quarrelling I heard—

Alex I thought you said you heard the car start up *after* all the commotion?

Dinah It must have been before—I don't remember exactly.

Alex (*starting to pace about the room*) All right, I realize I *may* appear to be the victim of incriminating circumstances, but there *has* to be a logical explanation. (*He stops and turns*) I've been framed!

Dinah How appropriate—framed for the murder of an artist!

Alex (*pacing again*) I can't think of anyone who could hate me so much.

Dinah Try looking in *Who's Who*?

Alex Your concern is touching.

Dinah Alex, you're irritating me, stalking about the room like a wounded tiger. No-one is trying to frame you because you murdered them both. (*She heads for the desk*) I'm sorry, but I'm going to call the police.

Alex (*rushing to intercept Dinah*) The police?

Dinah (*calmly*) Damned little point my calling the fire brigade.

Alex That was *my* line.

Dinah picks up the telephone receiver

Why didn't you spill the beans to Weaver when he came back?

Dinah I wasn't absolutely sure then—I am now.

Alex But, you'd have to confess that you shot Tony.

Dinah Yes, but since the shot I fired obviously didn't kill him, that puts me in the clear, doesn't it? It lets me off the hook. I'll explain everything—that

I shot Tony believing him to be the prowler you warned me of—because he was about to attack me. I'll say I only fired a warning shot, that I didn't kill him—you did, then you strangled Cathy with your tie because you were terrified she'd report you to the police. The evidence is overwhelmingly against you.

Alex But—I'd be charged with murder—

Dinah We can't simply throw her body over the cliff and pretend nothing happened, can we?

Alex I'd get *twenty* years to life!

Dinah Enough time for you to write your memoirs. With good behaviour, if that's ever possible where you're concerned, you might be out for your seventieth birthday—we could throw a "welcome home" party at the Darby and Joan club. (*She starts to dial*)

Alex (*protesting*) But I am *in-no-cent*!

Dinah I'm sorry Alex, but I gotta call the cops.

Alex (*desperately cutting off the call*) Wait—look, last night, when you thought *you'd* killed Tony—when you were in the same situation, I agreed to cover for you—I lied to Weaver to protect you. I did that because—(*an embarrassing admission*)—because I still love you.

Dinah (*unmoved*) So now you want me to return the compliment?

Alex (*calmer*) Well, fair's fair.

Dinah (*replacing the receiver*) I have a position to uphold in society. (*She paces the room*) I am nationally famous—I'm due to appear on breakfast television next month—did I tell you?

Alex I'll be sure to watch.

Dinah (*continuing*) My readers would never expect such a compromise from me. I have my duty to the Crown as a law-abiding citizen—

Alex I think I get the message—

Dinah It would haunt my conscience for the rest of my life—I don't think I could live with the knowledge—

Alex (*interrupting*) I'd make it worth your while—

Dinah (*stopping*) What *exactly* do you mean?

Alex You've quickly abandoned your guilty conscience.

Dinah That's because I can be a very compassionate person.

Alex If—if you agree to keep quiet about all this, I'll restore half your allowance.

Dinah (*heading straight for the telephone*) I'm not kinda wild about that idea. (*She picks up the receiver*)

Alex All right, I'll forget about last night's agreement and continue to pay you your full allowance.

Dinah (*hesitating*) *Now* you're begining to interest me.

Alex Only "beginnning to"?

Dinah What you pay me now hardly covers my weekly shopping bill at Fortnum and Mason's.

Alex (*incredulous*) Fortnam and Mason's? Why can't you go to the supermarket like everyone else?

Dinah They never have anchovies or prune yoghurt at the supermarket.

Alex (*realizing he is defeated*) What's your deal?

Dinah (*thinking for a moment*) Double my allowance and I'll call it square.

Alex *Double* it?—That's ludicrous.

Dinah (*clearly enjoying herself, mimicking Cathy's accent*) Not as ludicrous as my calling the forty-fifth precinct.

Alex I don't have that kind of money—there wouldn't be anything left for me.

Dinah I'd let you keep Cathy's paintings.

Alex (*sulkily*) Great.

Dinah And the cottage.

Alex (*gloomily*) I didn't know you could be so generous.

Dinah (*waving the telephone receiver*) Do I call them or not?

Alex Oh all right, Have your pound of flesh. It's a deal. Discount for prompt payment?

Dinah (*replacing the receiver*) You can merely reflect in the glory of my not exposing you as the ruthless killer you are. I'll have my solicitor draw up fresh papers.

Alex Yes, let's have it all legal—don't want any misunderstandings, do we?

Dinah Of course not. What are you going to do with Cathy's body?

Alex I'll move it tonight—after it's dark. Can't risk doing it now in case some of Weaver's cronies are watching the house. (*Reflecting*) At least Tony will have a more dignified send-off—the grave of the unknown inventor. What puzzles me is—who switched the bullets?—

Dinah Alex, must you persist with—

Alex (*persisting*) The gun was loaded with blanks and I just can't believe Cathy would have switched the bullets.

Dinah And now you'll never find out, will—(*hesitating*) what do you mean, the gun was loaded with blanks?

Alex Yes, I simply can't—

Dinah *Blanks?* Yesterday, when I was handling the gun you told me to be careful because it was loaded, so what's this about switching bullets?

Alex (*realizing he's just slipped up*) I—I—

Dinah Why would you have? (*Resuming pacing the room*) Why should you have—(*realizing a startling possibility*)—you callous, cold-blooded treacherous—

Alex Dinah—

Dinah You knew all the time, didn't you? You planned the whole thing—arranged the entire set-up. You *knew* I would shoot Tony.

Alex (*moving towards Dinah*) Don't be ridiculous, how could I possibly know you would shoot him? I'm not psychic.

Dinah I'm beginning to get a very clear picture. You put the gun where I would easily find it—if I hadn't left my lighter in the office—I remember now, I *did* put my lighter in my bag before I left the office. You must have removed it from my bag just after I got here—no wonder you made me go and hang up my own coat. (*She holds out her hand*) Would you kindly return my lighter, please?

Alex (*heading for the buffet*) All right Dinah, you win. I *do* have your lighter—it's in my jacket pocket—I'll get it for you later. (*He mixes a drink*)

Dinah (*reflecting*) Your story about the prowler—there wasn't a prowler, was there? You invented him to have me believe Tony was the prowler. It's—it's almost like the plot from one of your thrillers ... perhaps *too* much like the plot from *Calibre*.

Alex turns

No wonder you were both so goddamned startled when you found I was reading the very book on which you'd based your plan. (*Now mimicking Alex*) "The butler did it! Poison in the French onion soup".

Alex (*coming downstage with his drink*) Brown Windsor soup, actually.

Dinah And *if* I remember correctly, I had a book of matches from the "Green Pagoda" restaurant in my bag. (*She opens her bag and searches it thoroughly*) Well, what do you know? That's missing as well, or rather, you planted it in Tony's pocket. I wonder how long it will be before the police find the gun in my flat. Where did you hide it—behind the rubber plant or in the deep freeze?

Alex (*after a swift swig of his drink*) If it will help convince you of my innocence, I moved the gun this morning—before you came down—just in case you had ideas about wiping it clean of fingerprints to destroy my evidence against you.

Dinah Why all the intricate plotting simply to avoid having to pay my allowance? It couldn't have been just for that—that Tony had to die.

Alex Tony, that scientific wizard and creator of countless useless inventions, had finally come up with a winner. We were ready to register the patent—expected it would gross at least a million in the first year but—I had *one* small problem—I'd have to pay half my share of the profits to you. Rather unfair, don't you think, since it was *my* money which financed the whole project.

Dinah It might seem unfair to you, but an agreement is an agreement, which rational people honour, no matter what the inequalities.

Alex (*raising his glass in a toast*) Spoken like a true sob columnist.

Dinah *Don't* call me a sob columnist—you know I resent that description. I happen to take great solace form my work.

Alex Okay, don't bark. Only said in jest. Anyway, I *had* to find a way to get out of paying you my share of the proceeds, so we devised a plan and ... well, you know the rest. The outcome was, however, unforeseen.

Dinah So, Tony made his grand entrance through the french windows purporting to be an assailant?

Alex You were supposed to shoot him, think he was dead. I'd loaded the gun with blanks—like we used for the rehearsals—

Dinah (*incredulously*) *You had rehearsals?*

Alex To ensure that everything was workable—

Dinah Full dress rehearsals? My God! Incredible, absolutley incredible. You lured me here to prey on my *one* weakness, and I suppose if my car hadn't so conveniently broken down, you had some neat trick up your sleeve to have me stranded here for the night. Alfred Hitchcock, eat your heart out!

Alex (*almost standing to attention*) I consider it an honour to be classed in the same mode as the Master!

Dinah Alex, your actions belong in the gutter. How could you even think about such a despicable act?

Alex It—came to me.

Dinah Yes, I was forgetting—*Calibre* and like you said, the ending was *very* disappointing. Just to put my mind *completely* at ease, I would like custody of the gun.

Alex is silent

(*Firmly*) The gun, please.

Alex If I don't give it to you?

Dinah I call the police—and don't forget—we've still got to think up a plausible story which will explain why Tony's body is in my flat. I can *still* drop you right in it.

Alex (*putting his glass on the coffee table*) Oh, very well then. (*He goes to the bookcase, pulls out a thick volume and takes the gun from behind it, replaces the book, then turns to Dinah so that she can see the gun*) There, does *that* satisfy you I didn't place it somewhere in your flat?

Dinah You could have used a different gun.

Alex (*coming towards Dinah*) Why do you persist in trying to convince yourself of my guilt? Are you a self-appointed judge, jury—

Dinah And executioner?

Alex The death penalty *has* been abolished.

Dinah A great shame, with dangerous men like you around. Compared with you, Crippen was a saint.

Dinah reaches for the gun, which Alex gives her reluctantly, then he collects his glass from the coffee table and is about to take a sip when he sees Dinah aiming the gun at him. He cannot hide his puzzlement and surprise

Sit down, Alex.

Alex Dinah, What the—

Dinah I said sit down.

Alex (*putting his glass back on the coffee table and slowly sinking on to the sofa*) Don't be ridiculous—put that gun away, it's only loaded with blanks.

Dinah (*with a sinister tone*) Try telling that to Tony.

Alex Dinah, are you out of your mind?

Dinah There is one remaining item on the agenda.

Alex I swear, I don't have your key ring. You *must* have left it at—

Dinah Don't play dumb, Alex. The plans.

Alex What plans?

Dinah (*still pointing the gun at Alex*) Plans, details, specifications, whatever—for Tony's remarkable invention. I want them.

Alex (*rising*) I'm not letting you have those.

Dinah (*pointing the gun more purposefully*) I told you to sit down.

Alex does as instructed

Your game is over, *finis*. You killed Tony so that you could register the patent in your sole name and claim *all* the rights under it.

Alex I can't let you have the plans—

Dinah Darling, I'm afraid you don't have any choice.

Alex I don't have them—Tony had them.

Dinah (*motioning with the gun*) You're lying!
Alex (*about to rise*) Dinah—
Dinah Stay where you are.

Alex relaxes

Good, now, tell me all about those plans.
Alex But why? What possible use can they be to you?
Dinah I'll claim the patent myself, why do you think? I might as well take full advantage of the situation in which I find myself.
Alex (*rising but keeping away from Dinah*) How could *you* claim the patent? I have copies, so you wouldn't be able to claim the patent without *my* consent— and I'm certainly not going to give that—*and* don't overlook the fact that Tony also had copies which will pass to his estate after probate—
Dinah Don't fool with me, Alex. I know very well that if anything, you are thorough, and since you'd planned to double-cross your partner, it's obvious you would have taken great care to have obtained *all* the copies. Now, you either tell me where they are or—I use this weapon—don't forget I got the hang of how to fire it last night.
Alex (*starting to move towards Dinah*) I'm going to call your bluff!

Dinah cocks the gun, aims it at Alex's head

(*Stopping dead*) On second thoughts!

Dinah lowers the gun and secures it

Dinah You were telling me where the plans were?
Alex Was I?

Dinah is still looking hostile

They're in the wall safe upstairs. I'll get them for you. (*He starts to go towards the staircase*)
Dinah Hold it right there! I will get them.
Alex But—you don't know the combination to the safe.
Dinah I will in a moment—write it down for me.

Dinah motions Alex to the desk with the gun. Alex goes to the desk

And don't try anything—remember, I've got you covered!

Alex writes the combination on the notepad, using Dinah's pen, then puts the pen down, tears off the page aggressively, and hands it to Dinah, under her watchful eye

This had better be the correct number. (*She puts the note in her pocket*)
Alex (*moving C*) It is, I'm through playing games with you.
Dinah I guess—(*she corrects herself*) I suppose that's everything then. (*She raises the gun as if to shoot Alex*)
Alex Dinah! What the—what now?
Dinah (*keeping a safe distance from Alex*) What now? I'm sorry Alex, but the time has come for me to—make the divorce absolute!

Alex (*terrified*) Dinah, for God's sake—don't be a fool!

Dinah As I said—I need a plausible story for Weaver. I'll tell him *exactly* what happened. How you tried to con me into thinking *I'd* killed Tony. How you took his body to my flat. How you murdered Cathy and were about to kill me when I threatened to expose you—I shot you in self-defence! (*She is poised, ready to fire*)

Alex (*a petrified ruin*) Dinah, *no, please*—

Dinah moves slowly to the front of the sofa, nearer Alex, as if to be certain she won't miss when she shoots at him. Alex has all but fainted from fright, then Dinah collapses on to the sofa laughing uncontrollably

Dinah (*eventually*) You thought I'd do it! You really thought I was going to shoot you—(*rising*)—to fill you full of lead! (*She bursts into laughter again*)

Alex (*mightily relieved*) Dinah, that little performance was in very bad taste.

Dinah If you could have seen your face! God, I've waited ten years for that! You were reduced to a vulnerable, defeated victim—just like I was last night. You looked so pathetic, I just *had* to give you a reprieve!

Alex (*shaking his head*) Why, Dinah, why?

Dinah I wanted *you* to know just how Tony must have felt last night, when he had to gaze down the barrel. I want you to have to live with the horror of that moment for the rest of your life. It's only right that you should after what you have done.

Alex I keep telling you—*I didn't kill him!* (*Thinking*) Look I'll prove I didn't. Give me the gun.

Dinah Oh no, I'm not falling for that trick.

Alex All right then—open up the chamber.

Dinah motions for Alex to keep away from her, and opens the chamber

How many bullets are there in the chamber?

Dinah (*checking the chamber*) Five.

Alex Then Tony *couldn't* have been shot twice with *that* gun—if he had been, there would only be *four* bullets left.

Dinah (*closing the chamber*) Hmm, unless you replaced one bullet to have me believe that.

Alex Why do you have to challenge my every defence?

Dinah (*putting the gun in her pocket*) You don't understand do you? You simply don't understand.

Alex Understand what? I did not leave the cottage last night and commit those horrifying murders—not unless I've taken to sleep-walking.

Dinah Not sleep-walking Alex, something deeper and more sinister—

Alex Dinah, what are you talking about?

Dinah You've lost control of yourself. You don't control yourself any more, Alex.

Alex That's absurd—

Dinah Is it?

Alex is silent

It's difficult for me to try and explain—but I was researching the very subject recently for a feature article I was working on. The problem is, Alex, that you have become the victim of a strange and evil force—a mysterious phenomena which nobody can yet fully explain. It's like a sort of self-hypnosis—that completely unknown to yourself, you have been taken over by the characters in your murder thrillers.

Alex How totally ridiculous—

Dinah (*continuing*) You perform all the acts they do—you live *their* lives. Last night, you became one of the characters from the book on which you based your ploy. You lived the part—the part of a murderer!

Alex (*shocked*) No!

Dinah Yes Alex, by day you are husband, neighbour, golfing partner—you are Alex Conrad who we all know and despise, but by night—the transformation. A psychopathic killer!

Alex (*wandering in a daze*) That can't be—that can't be—

Dinah *Think* Alex, what other explanation is there?

Alex (*turning to Dinah*) I—I don't know.

Dinah You didn't have control of yourself. You were not fully aware of your actions. An alien body was dominating you—you couldn't help yourself.

Alex Oh my God! Oh sweet Jesus!

Dinah The first thing to do Alex, is *please* get rid of all those books. (*She points to the bookcase*) Sell the whole collection.

Alex picks up his glass. His hands are trembling. Sell the collection? A difficult decision to make, perhaps the most difficult he has ever had to make

Alex If—if you think it will help. (*He takes a sip of his drink*)

Dinah I think it will help a great deal. (*She goes to the bottom of the staircase*) I think it's time I changed out of these things, and I think it would be a good idea if you cleaned the bloodstains from the carpet.

Alex Yes, I will.

Dinah climbs the staircase then stops and turns

Dinah Strange isn't it? You devise a very clever ploy and yet become the victim of it yourself. Now it seems *I'm* holding all the trump cards.

She continues up the staircase and exits

Alex (*considering his drink*) Not—necessarily.

The lights fade to—

Black-out

SCENE 3

The same. Late that evening

When the Lights come up it is late evening; the curtains at the french windows are pulled half-closed and the room's lamps are lighted. Dinah, wearing her

two-piece again, is slowly pacing the room downstage, and smoking a cigarette.
The french windows are closed, but Alex appears outside after a moment, lets
himself in through the doors, then closes them behind him. He is about to
lock the doors when he realizes the key is missing from the lock

Dinah *(turning)* The bereaved lover returns.

Alex *(ignoring the comment)* Have you seen the key to these doors? It's missing.

Dinah I've no idea where it is—you probably misplaced it as a result of last
night's capers.

Alex Yes, maybe. *(He closes the curtains and comes downstage, rubbing his*
hands) It's turning chilly out there—could be a frost in the morning. Fix
me a drink, will you?—And one for yourself.

Dinah *(stubbing out her cigarette in the ashtray)* Scotch? *(She goes to the*
buffet)

Alex Please. You have whatever you want.

Dinah *(mixing the drinks)* What have you done with Cathy's body?

Alex *(solemnly)* It's disposed of.

Dinah Two bodies within twenty-four hours—not bad going considering the
moon isn't even full. *(She comes downstage with the drinks)*

Alex Your remorse is touching. *(Taking his drink from Dinah)* Cheers.

Dinah *(raising her glass)* To—absent friends?

Alex *(still solemnly)* . . . absent friends.

They both take tentative sips of their drinks

Dinah Where did you put Cathy's body? Did you bury it?

Alex Don't worry, I haven't left it in your flat. It won't be discovered this
time—and you have *my* word on that. *(He sinks on to the sofa)* God, I couldn't
believe what I was doing out there. I *still* can't believe I'm responsible for
all that's happened. It's like I've lived through a grim and ghastly nightmare.

Dinah You did—in a manner of speaking.

Alex Honestly, Dinah, I really am distraught and shattered over all this. When
everything has blown over, I think I'll do voluntary work for the Samaritans.

Dinah *(sternly)* Alex, I *don't* think that would be a good idea.

Alex No? It's just that I feel—

Dinah If you *really* feel so badly about everything, I can give you an address
you can write to for help—

Alex Please don't treat me like one of the letters in your pending tray.

Dinah I was only trying to help.

Alex *(rising)* I guess I'm—Oh God, now I'll have to stop saying that. I suppose
I'm in a state of after-shock. *(Trying to pull himself together)* You took
your time getting back, I expected you hours ago—wasn't your car ready?

Dinah I stopped by the hotel for dinner.

Alex Why did you go to the hotel? There's enough food in the house.

Dinah I didn't fancy what was left of Cathy's meatloaf. Has that Inspector
telephoned yet?

Alex Not that I know of—he might have rung while I was—moving the body.

Dinah That poor girl—I simply can't believe you did it.

Alex *(a little firmly)* Neither can I. The more I think about what you told me—about my sub-conscience and not having control of myself—the more I feel it just wasn't possible—

Dinah Alex, I explained fully what the symptoms are and how they—

Alex (*interrupting*) Let's suppose just for a moment, that I *didn't* kill them both. What other explanation is there? What for example, is *your* alibi? After all, *you* lied to the Inspector as well.

Dinah I lied to protect you.

Alex He was extremely interested in *your* activities last night— (*thinking*) and there was a six-hour period last night where I can't account for your movements. You had as much opportunity as I to have driven to your flat with Tony's body. The return journey only takes about four hours—less at that time of night with hardly any traffic about and your foot on the gas.

Dinah What, risk being stopped for speeding, with a dead body in the boot?

Alex You could have got there and back within four hours without having to break the limit.

Dinah And motive? What about a motive? You'd already agreed to cover for me and dispose of Tony's body, so why would I wish to incriminate myself further by taking his body to my own flat, and murdering Cathy?

Alex An elaborate double-bluff! To make out you'd been framed! If the police believed that, they'd know I was the only suspect, and since it was *my* gun that was used in the shooting—at least, the first shooting, you'd have had me where you've always wanted me. In gaol! *And* your allowance restored. Very clever Dinah, very clever. *Almost* like a plot from one of my books.

Dinah I'm not *that* devious. Why would I have killed Cathy?

Alex You were madly jealous that a younger and more attractive woman was in love with me.

Dinah Alex, you are talking absolute nonsense. Your theory is interesting but wholly inaccurate, as you well realize. You are entirely responsible for this gruesome sequence of events, so it's no good you trying to transfer your guilt to me. Since our numbers have diminished rapidly since last night, I'd like to return home as soon as possible, so would you mind ringing my flat to see if that Inspector is still there, and find out when it will be all right for me to go back? (*She puts her glass on the coffee table*) I'm going to freshen myself up.

Dinah exits upstairs

Alex goes to the phone with his drink and dials a nine-digit number

Alex (*on the phone*) . . . Who is that please? . . . Sergeant Brownlee? This is Mr Conrad . . . yes, that's right. Is Inspector Weaver there, please? . . . Oh, no, nothing important, my wife asked me to ring to find out when it will be in order for her to return . . . Yes, I understand, I'll tell her, What? . . . Er, no, I still haven't found the gun—I've searched high and low . . . Yes, I will . . . Goodbye. (*He replaces the receiver and goes DC taking a sip of his drink. He stands in front of the sofa thinking*)

After a few moments, the sound of the sea can be heard and the curtains blow inward. Alex is oblivious to the sound at first, then turns to face the french windows as it stops, and the curtains settle

(*Warily*) Dinah—is that you?

There is silence. Alex puts his glass on the coffee table and starts to go upstage

Badger enters from behind the curtains. He is a dishevelled tramp and it is difficult to assess his age. His unkempt hair and neglected beard are a mess, and he is wearing a torn and raggy old raincoat, secured by a piece of string. He has a dirty scarf around his neck, and his fingers show through the ends of his gloves. He has a slight limp in his left leg and he speaks with something like a West Country accent

Alex stares at him in disbelief

Badger (*coming into the room*) Evenin', guv.
Alex (*unable to hide his surprise*) Who—who the devil are you?
Badger Just yer friendly neighbourhood tramp—
Alex I don't believe this!
Badger (*coming nearer to Alex*) People calls me Badger.

Alex appraises the tramp, speechless

Sorry to barge in on yer like—
Alex Get out of here! (*He points to the french windows*)
Badger It's a wee bit cold out there ternight an' I was 'opin yer could spare a poor old soul some board an' lodgings. 'Aven't eaten owt since yesterday, 'part from an odd carrot 'ave dug up from yon farms.
Alex (*angrily*) I told you to get out—or would you rather I called the police?
Badger I wouldn't be doin' that, guv.
Alex (*puzzled*) Give me *one* good reason why I shouldn't. And *don't* call me "guv".
Badger I seen too much, guv.
Alex ... what do you mean?
Badger (*running his hand along one side of the sofa*) Beautiful, real beautiful. (*He comes round to the front of the sofa, sits on it and bounces up and down on it a couple of times*) 'Aven't slept on owt like this fer years.
Alex (*coming to the front of the sofa*) I asked, what do you mean, you've seen too much? And kindly get the hell off my upholstery.
Badger I knows what's been goin' on 'ere. (*He picks up a cushion and starts plumping it to test the quality*)
Alex (*uneasily*) Go on ...
Badger (*putting the cushion down*) I just seen yer carry the body of that young girl out and bury it. Real pretty girl—she the one what's been 'anging around 'ere? (*He wanders around the room to inspect what to him are untold luxuries*)
Alex How do you know that?
Badger Been 'anging around these parts meself for a few weeks now. Pinching a few chickens from that farm down yon. (*Pauses*) Why'd yer kill the girl?
Alex I didn't kill her.
Badger Dear, dear, dear—I knows what 'appens 'ere last night—sees it all through a gap in them curtains. (*He motions towards the french windows*)
Alex Just what *did* happen here last night?

Badger spots the buffet, picks up a decanter, wipes the top of it with one hand, takes a swig directly from it, then belches

Badger Come on guv, you don't need me to tell yer.

Alex looks shaken, while Badger takes another swig, wipes his mouth with one hand, then puts the decanter down

Don't look so shaken guv, I'm not one what gossips . . . Not unless—

Alex (*moving towards Badger*) Not unless—what?

Badger You knows 'ow it is, guv. 'Ave nowhere to go, 'as ter sleep rough every night, find what scraps er food I can. 'Cept when I finds me the occasional chicken—

Alex Oh, if it's food you want, I have some meatloaf left over—

Badger I was thinking about something more fulfilling—

Alex Will you tell me what it is you want, then go?

Badger (*continuing his exploration of the room*) Well guv, it's like this. 'Ave never 'armed no one—'ave never asked for much, but 'ave not 'ad no luck in this life. (*He starts to reflect on his life*) Things started well enough—got me a nice wife—ar was a good enough looking bloke when ar was young—nice 'ouse. Then the accident—that wer' what started it all. 'It an' run it was—ar was in 'ospital six months, nearly seven. Enid—that was me wife—came to visit me at first—then (*sadly*) met another bloke—went off with 'im—ar never saw 'er again. Lost me 'ouse, everything—*and* me job, wi' being in 'ospital ser long. Nearly lost me leg—just saved in time, but 'ave still got the limp. Never found the driver what run me over—so—'ave 'ad to scrape 'and ter mouth ever since.

Alex (*having listened with some interest*) Your circumstances are most tragic but hardly *my* responsibility. Have you tried the Department of Health and Social Security?

Badger No-one wants ter know me. Am an outcast, a pestilence on society, a vermin best rid of an' forgotton about.

Alex You 'ave—(*correcting himself*)—you have my heart-felt sympathy.

Badger So a few bob wouldn't go amiss.

Alex If it's money you want, I'm afraid you're ill-luck must continue, because I don't have any.

Badger Give us a break, guv. Nice warm-'earted country gent like yerself. 'Ave never asked for much in this life, ar don't cause no bother . . . Ar don't want to *cause* no bother.

Alex Am I to understand that you intend to blackmail me?

Badger What's—blackmail, guv?

Alex Money extorted under the threat of exposure.

Badger Yes, then ar be a-blackmailing yer.

Alex If I don't pay?

Badger S'pose 'al just 'ave to gossip down at t'local nick—well-known there, sometimes 'as to stay the night.

Alex What exactly will you tell them at the—local nick? (*He moves slowly towards the desk*)

Badger Like ar says—'ave seen everything through them windows—you wasn't very—careful, was yer?

Alex If I give you a fiver, will you shove off?

Badger It's not that am one what's greedy guv, but am sure an expensive gent like yerself can raise a more rewarding donation.

Alex *(moving towards the desk)* A fiver's about all the spare cash I have—the rest of my wealth is tied up in capital assets.

Badger *(enquiring)* I don't know what yer be a-meaning, not being properly educated like. *(He is now at the rear of the sofa between the alcove and the french windows)*

Alex Just tell me how much you want.

Badger Well, it's like this—what'd yer reckon's fair?

Alex A tenner's my limit.

Badger Ten's fine.

Alex *(relieved)* Splendid, I'll just get you—

Badger If you add three noughts on to the end.

Alex Three noughts—*(he calculates)*—that's ten grand. *(He discreetly picks up the paper-knife)*

Badger Yer wouldn't ever see me again—

Alex You're out of your mind—look, I can take a joke, but you're beginning to make me very angry, and when I get angry I'm likely to—

Badger The longer you delay, the more it goes up.

Alex becomes very hostile, moves swiftly towards Badger, the paper-knife raised

Alex Why, you filthy, miserable vagrant—

Badger *(pulling a revolver from his pocket and aiming it at Alex)* Drop that knife!

Alex stops in his tracks, completely surprised

Ar said—drop the knife!

Alex drops the knife. (NOTE: He must drop it where he can grab it very quickly)

That's better—didn't think you'd want to be a responsible for *three* murders, guv.

Alex Where did you get that gun?

Badger comes round to the front of the sofa, keeping the revolver aimed at Alex

Badger Don't seem you're a-getting the message.

Alex moves slowly to the side of the sofa R, keeping a wary eye on the revolver

What ar knows could put yer away for life—

Alex You can't possibly know—

Badger So the time's come for us to be practical, like.

Alex There isn't anything you can pin on me, so put that toy away.

Badger I think you'll find it's real.

Alex *(thinking)* I could give you a cheque—

Badger pulls off his wig and false beard. Tony has risen from the grave

Tony But—I don't have a bank account! (*He throws the beard and wig on to the sofa*)

Alex (*more than astonished*) Tony!

Tony Please—no applause.

Alex You're supposed to be—

Tony Dead? Yes, I know. What do you think of this unexpected development—this startling twist?

Alex (*very much relieved*) This is incredible ... Thank God you're alive, you can't begin to know what I've been through today. This is a miracle!

Tony Not quite a miracle guv—or rather—*old boy*. Tony has not risen from the dead. I knew you would switch the bullets, so naturally, I took precautions.

Alex I didn't switch bullets—I never intended switching the bullets. (*He moves towards Tony*)

Tony (*aiming the revolver purposefully*) Tell that to the angels.

Alex Since you don't seem to believe me, *you* have some explaining to do. Dinah and I have almost drawn swords over you. Who the hell's body is it in her flat? We've had the police here—Detective Inspector Weaver—

Tony Ah, yes, Detective Inspector Weaver, the intrepid investigator—the bull-dog!

Alex You—you know Weaver?

Tony My cousin Tarquin—haven't I ever mentioned him to you? Part-time actor—prominent thespian, strictly amateur of course. Currently masquerading, I understand, as one Sergeant Brownlee. He's at Dinah's flat, but as the mystery is now solved, I think I ought to call him and officially take him off the case.

Alex You despicable toad!

Tony Manners, old boy, manners.

Alex Why all the cloak-and-dagger stuff? Why the tramp performance?

Tony (*putting the revolver in his pocket*) It's like this, old boy—(*moving about left*) You kind of got me hooked into thrillers—the twists and turns, the shady characters, the reversal of situations, and since I owe you one—

Alex Owe me one?

Tony Yes. My last patent—the one we were beaten to the market with—or so you told me, and had me believe. We weren't beaten at all, were we? You claimed it as your own and tricked—no, *swindled* me out of my rightful share. (*He takes off his scarf and gloves and throws them on the sofa*)

Alex I protest over that shameful allegation—

Tony (*cutting him off sharply*) It took me some time before I caught on to your deceit. Why your sudden interest in art, I asked myself.

Alex Did you tell yourself the answer?

Tony I gradually worked things out. I first became suspicious when I read a report in a trade journal about some marvellous new invention which was about to take off—the problem was—there was one *tiny* flaw in the specifications which was delaying things. A tiny flaw—something seemed familiar about it, so I checked over my original specs and—magic, I'd made the same mistake! Too much of a coincidence. That unknown to us and at the very same time, someone else was developing the identical idea and made the identical mistake. That's when I became interested in *your* interest in art.

Alex Tony, I have never heard so much—

Tony (*again cutting him off sharply*) Take a close look at the painting above the buffet.

Alex goes to the buffet, scrutinizes the painting, then turns

Alex Where's the original?

Tony In safe custody. I switched it last night.

Alex Will you come to the point.

Tony Clever, very clever. You buy a genuine Claude Vincente picture—what's it worth? Quarter of a million? You have Cathy make you a copy—same initials, 'CV', but that picture is different. Cathy usually signed her full name—but not on that one—it's just signed 'CV'. That's when I first became suspicious. You should have destroyed Cathy's replica—not left it lying around the loft, where I found it after much searching.

Alex I congratulate you on an excellent piece of deduction. (*He mixes a drink*)

Tony Why a painting?

Alex Cathy always thought it was her reproduction on the wall. She did the copy from a book of Vincente's work. When the time came to sell it, all I'd need to do was convince you I'd hit lucky with one of her paintings.

Tony And the rest of the money?

Alex (*hesitates*) Switzerland.

Tony Why Switzerland?

Alex 'Cause they gave me a free plastic carrier for opening the account, why do you think, dummy? (*He takes a swig of his drink*)

Tony You have behaved rather badly, old boy. Deceit, tax evasion—I don't think the Inland Revenue will think too kindly of you.

Alex (*moving slowly downstage*) Okay—I admit I double-crossed you last time. Dinah was milking me for everything I had, but—let's settle this small indiscretion.

Tony I don't describe one million pounds sterling as a small indiscretion.

Alex You can have full rights to the new patent.

Tony What new patent?

Alex The one you've just completed—the one we've gone to all the trouble over.

Tony Christ, you haven't caught on have you? There isn't any new patent, you dum-dum. I've set you up!

Alex Set me up?

Tony Like I said, I'm hooked on thrillers. I've slowly worked my way through the greater part of your magnificent library, picking up odd ideas here, workable twists there, until I was able to formulate my plan. I knew that if I dangled the carrot, you'd take the bait.

Alex Like pinning Cathy's murder on me.

Tony The evidence—

Alex The fabricated evidence. Why all that?

Tony To frighten and confuse you. Hasty thinking equals mistakes and errors of judgement. I wanted to play and beat you at your own game. I think I have succeeded admirably. First, Detective Inspector Weaver—

Alex A bogus detective—straight out of *Sleuth*.

Tony (*forcefully*) Weaver was *my* creation. Then—the *real* victim of the crime—Cathy.

Alex (*coming towards Tony*) You murdering bastard!

Tony (*taking out the gun, aiming it at Alex*) That's far enough.

Alex Why Cathy? You didn't have to kill the girl. She knew nothing about my reasons for the painting.

Tony I feel no remorse. She never liked me—she wanted me dead—I overheard her trying her damnedest to persuade you to switch the bullets—not that you *did* need any persuading.

Alex I'll kill you for that, Tony.

Tony I think not. It was your fault she had to die—that delectable Floridian Venus! But then—what good's a thriller if there isn't a skeleton in the cupboard? Or did Inspector Weaver use that line?

Alex You're a sick man, Tony—but I know someone who may be able to help you.

Tony Ah yes, where is the Queen of the gossip columns?

Alex Upstairs powdering her nose—she'll be down in another hour or so.

Tony That still gives me plenty of time. Tell me, was Tarquin—I mean the Inspector—convincing.

Alex He had me going some, I admit, but take my advice, he has no future as a detective—has a habit of missing salient clues.

Tony Like?

Alex All the tit-bits you planted—bloodstained carpets, spent bullets, *bodies* falling out of cupboards.

Tony Bodies falling out of cupboards?

Alex Don't worry he didn't see anything—but what is he going to tell the police when he's figured out what really happened?

Tony I don't think he'll be rushing to tell them anything. He's had a couple of brushes with the law already over drugs—he's the black sheep of the family. And what would he tell them? That he impersonated a police officer?

Alex You've worked everything out perfectly, haven't you?

Tony After much careful and meticulous planning. Now be honest, how was *my* performance? Tarquin has been coaching me into how to deliver lines and time the funnies.

Alex You were quite superb—nearly had me in tears with all that family crap—and the costume—a sensation.

Tony Courtesy of Moss Bros.

Alex (*checking his watch*) If you've only paid the hire charge up to midnight, you've got about one hour left before you turn into a pumpkin.

Tony remains silent

Well, is that it, or is there one more scene?

Tony We've almost reached the final curtain.

Alex Don't tell me there's another twist to come. Why all the cloak-and-dagger stuff? Why didn't you simply shoot me weeks ago and have done with it?

Tony That would have been too—anti-climatic.

Alex So what's next?—the suspense is killing me.

Tony What's next is—the time has come for me to dissolve the partnership. I am going to kill you.

Alex OK, I've taken your point, now stop playing at Al Capone and put that gun away. We can work out a deal—I'll sell the painting—give you your share—how's that?

Tony (*cocking the revolver*) I'm serious about this, old boy. Deadly serious. It is customary to allow the condemned prisoner a last request. Any last requests?

Alex How about "We'll Meet Again"?

Tony I'd hoped you'd make a more dramatic plea. (*He pauses*) Sorry Alex, but it's time to say good-bye. (*He raises the revolver, ready to fire*)

Alex (*looking past Tony*) Ah, Inspector, just in time.

Tony Nice try, but you don't think I'd fall for that outdated trick, do you?

Alex Don't say I didn't warn you.

Tony half-looks around and at that very moment, Alex grabs the paper-knife, raising it ready to pounce, as Tony recovers from the distraction

Tony Too late, old boy! (*He shoots Alex*)

Alex slowly falls behind the sofa grabbing the top of it and dropping the paper-knife

Alex Why Tony ... (*a dying gasp*) ... why? (*He slumps behind the sofa, dead*)

Tony ... Why not? (*He stares at the body*)

Dinah slowly descends the staircase

Dinah Is he dead?

Tony I guess so.

Dinah (*coming into the room*) I—I didn't think you'd do it.

Tony (*coming DC*) Thought I'd chicken out at the last minute? Not me—I've planned this for a year—been over every move and possibility.

Dinah Those sleeping tablets worked? I slipped a couple into his wine.

Tony He was sleeping like a baby when I went to get his tie and hank. I'll have to ring Tarquin and tell him he can go home. Did he suspect anything?

Dinah No, but my heart missed a few beats when Cathy's body fell out of the cupboard, just as he was leaving.

Tony Are you *sure* he didn't see anything?

Dinah Positive.

Tony (*putting the revolver on the desk*) You're going to become a very rich woman. I can't understand why Alex never changed his will. The cottage will be yours. And the income from my patent, once his will is through probate. You *will* reimburse me my share?

Dinah A deal's a deal. I don't double-cross people like he did. I'll sell the cottage though—I don't think I'd like to return here, the place will probably be haunted.

Tony takes a holdall out of the large cupboard

You'll sell the Vincente painting?

Tony (*putting his tramp's gear into the holdall*) And thus recover the fortune from my patent? Yes, but I'll leave it a while—until this whole sordid affair has blown over. (*He takes off the raincoat and bundles it into the holdall. He is now wearing a jacket and a white open-neck shirt*) You have the combination of the safe? I'll need to recover the phoney plans I gave him.

Dinah (*taking a note out of her pocket*) Here. (*She hands it to Tony*) I think I over-played my scene with Alex.

Tony (*taking the holdall to the cupboard*) Oh? (*He puts the holdall in the cupboard?*)

Dinah He thought I was going to kill him—I wish you could have seen his face, his reactions. He was like a trapped animal.

Tony (*coming back DC*) Not a particularly memorable day for him, was it?

Dinah I had him totally convinced he'd killed you both, with all that rubbish about not being in control of himself, just like you said.

Tony Did Tarquin have him going as the fearless Inspector?

Dinah I don't ever recall having seen him so shaken, but you only just made that call in time—he was about to leave—I thought I would have to stall him.

Tony I rang at nine—on the dot. His watch must have been a fraction slow. (*Checking his watch*) I think it's time to call the police. Is there anything we've overlooked?

Dinah Alex burned all the evidence of your murder in the garden fire. The bedsheet, the fake log. He's cleaned out the flask of blood and the bloodstains from the carpet.

Tony I imagined he'd be most co-operative about that, since you were able to convince him he'd done it. What about the bullet I planted in the painting?

Dinah I dropped it down a drain in the village.

Tony Good thinking, so the only remaining evidence is that of the unfortunate Cathy?

Dinah (*hesitating*) Tony, you *are* sure the police will buy the story?

Tony When they find Cathy's body and do the forensic tests, they'll find shreads of Cathy's clothing on Alex. Since the evidence that Alex buried her body is not false, what else will they think? (*Pauses*) Your secretary will testify to all those desperate telephone calls I made to you, purporting to be Alex—

Dinah Yes, she certainly will.

Tony And Alex made a false report to the police about a prowler—they're bound to wonder what he was up to—they'll agree the balance of his mind was disturbed. A verdict of misadventure, or accidental death, don't you think?

Dinah Or justifiable homicide? Suspended sentence—anything more and I'll plead your case in my column.

Tony (*removing his jacket*) I'll cover his body as a mark of respect (*Feeling in one of the pockets*) Nearly forgot—the key. (*He takes out a key, hands it to Dinah, and drapes the jacket over Alex's body*)

Dinah puts the key in the lock to the french windows. Tony goes to the desk and picks up the telephone receiver

Here goes. (*He dials a number*) Hello, Police? ... Something terrible has happened ... I've just shot my partner ... Westerby, Tony Westerby ... Alex Conrad—at his cottage on High Ridge Lane ... yes, that's the one. I—didn't mean to kill him—I'm numb with shock. I only meant to fire a warning shot—he was going to stab his former wife with a paper-knife ... Yes, he has been lately, something to do with his divorce settlement I think ... No, we won't touch anything ... Oh, one other thing. I haven't seen his ladyfriend all evening. Can't find her anywhere, but her van is in the yard ... I hope he hasn't done anything ... Oh God! (*He breaks down as if in distress and replaces the receiver*) Great!

Dinah (*coming C*) Did they buy it?

Tony They will.

Dinah bursts into laughter

I hope you'll appear a little more distraught when the police arrive. There's a patrol car in the area—it will be here shortly. We're not to touch anything.

Dinah Would *we* tamper with evidence?

Now Tony bursts into laughter

It all worked perfectly. You'd have thought that with all the thrillers he's read, he would have suspected something, but he fell for it hook, line and—

Tony The problem with amateur sleuths is that they are not able to expect the unexpected. We left him enough clues—your car handily broken down to ensure you'd have to stay the night, then you so conveniently writing letters at the desk. The bullet in the painting, the missing key to the french windows, the muddy shoes—

Dinah Compliments of the storm—

Tony Yes, an unexpected but extremely useful special effect.

Dinah He was so rattled you wouldn't have believed it.

Tony You know something? I couldn't help but wonder if *you'd* go along with it. (*He sits on the sofa*) I had visions of you striking a deal with Alex, then not switching the bullets.

Dinah I told you—with me, a deal is a deal.

Tony I *know* you switched the bullets; I came in and checked the gun to be sure. It was loaded with blanks. You understand why I had to take that precaution?

Dinah I'd have done the same. (*She pauses*) Just *when* did you check the gun? You must have been discreet—I never saw you.

Tony I sneaked in while you were all having dinner—I heard you complaining about Cathy's meatloaf—she tried to poison me with it once.

Dinah I can imagine. So, you discovered I had played along with your plan as agreed, and—(*She stops, thinks*)—When did you say you checked the gun?

Tony While you were having dinner.

Dinah But—I didn't switch the bullets until *after* we had dinner.

Tony Before, after, what's the difference?

Dinah (*coming in front of Tony*) The difference is—if the gun was already loaded with blanks—I switched blanks for—blanks.

Tony (*thinking*) That can't be. We both knew Alex would switch the bullets— are you trying to say that he didn't?

Dinah Before leaving the gun out on the ledge for you, I must have re-loaded it with blanks—thinking them to be the real bullets—

Tony If that *is* right, I must have shot Alex with—

Dinah Blanks?

Tony (*starting to rise*) Don't you know the bloody difference between real bullets and—*Ahhhhh!*

Tony lets out a deathly scream as Alex springs from behind the sofa, grabs him round the neck with one arm and stabs him ferociously with the paper-knife with the other. Dinah screams in terror, then Tony slumps to one side, dead, his shirt a bloody mess, the paper-knife through his heart

Alex I think he was trying to say "blanks"!

Alex comes around the sofa R; Dinah backs away L, terrified

You both thought I would switch the bullets! Why doesn't anyone trust me?

Dinah stands as frozen as a statue, whimpering at the sight of Tony's body

Yes Dinah, the amateur sleuth has made his fatal mistake. He didn't expect the unexpected. Take a close look at the murder weapon. The knife is not a fake—it's for real. No more tomfoolery—the magic of the theatre will not come to his aid. That *was* the final curtain. He's dead, returned to his maker, removed from the electoral register. His own blood spilled—gee, I'll have to shampoo the carpet—So, my day of vengeance is here at last, and you've written your final column—though I predict that sales of your newspaper will soar dramatically on Monday. Not often there's an obituary on the front page.

Dinah (*a trapped victim*) What do you mean?

Alex Imagine the headline—"Dinah Conrad Slain in House of Death!"

Dinah gasps

In cahoots with my loyal and trusting partner indeed! The evil act done, and you have lost. No more luncheons at the "Green Pagoda" with tinsel-clad Julian; no more shopping for anchovies and prune yoghurt at the general store on Piccadilly; no television appearance—postponed indefinitely. (*He pulls his club tie from his pocket*) Murder weapon number two! That'll confuse the jury!

Dinah stares at the tie in horror

My club tie—removed from Cathy's nimble neck. (*He stretches the tie between both hands and closes in on Dinah*) It's my favourite tie—and it *does* so come in handy from time to time . . .

Dinah (*petrified*) Alex. . . for God's sake—

A police siren can be heard in the distance

Alex (*his final triumph*) Yes, Dinah . . . I know *exactly* how you feel—

Alex moves towards Dinah, poised to strangle her with his tie as—

the CURTAIN *falls*

FURNITURE AND PROPERTY LIST

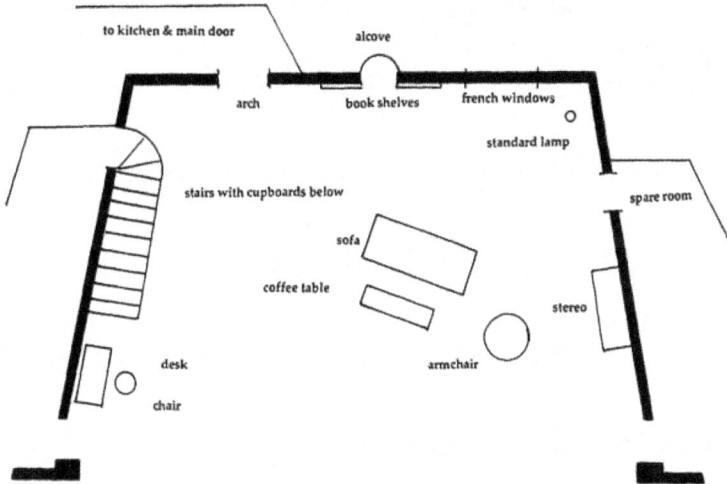

to kitchen & main door · alcove · arch · book shelves · french windows · standard lamp · stairs with cupboards below · spare room · sofa · coffee table · stereo · desk · armchair · chair

ACT I

SCENE I

On stage: Staircase. *Under it:* large storage cupboard. *In it:* broom, muddy shoes, holdall.
   Small storage cupboard
   Bookshelves filled with books (detective novels)
   Buffet. *On it:* drinks decanters, glasses, ice bucket, etc.
   Three abstract paintings
   Curtains over French windows
   Carpet
   Desk. *On it:* lamp, telephone, notepad. *In it:* gun, paper-knife, pen, notepaper,
      envelopes
   Swivel chair
   Standard lamp
   Armchair
   Sofa with cushions
   Coffee table. *On it:* ash tray, newspaper, glass

Off stage: Abstract painting (**Cathy**)

Personal: **Alex:** club tie, handkerchief, cigarette lighter, watch
   Cathy: watch
   Tony: watch

SCENE 2

Personal: **Dinah:** coat, shoulder bag (with cigarettes, lighter and pen inside)

SCENE 3

Off stage: "Log" [plans] (**Tony**)
          Bloodied bedsheet (**Cathy**)

Personal: **Dinah:** book (*Calibre*)

ACT II

SCENE 1

Check: Bedsheet crumpled in a heap in front of sofa

Set: Bullet lodged in painting above hi-fi equipment
           Cathy in closet, "wearing" Alex's tie and hankie

Personal: **Weaver:** notebook, watch

SCENE 2

Set: Gun behind a book on shelf

SCENE 3

Personal: **Tony:** gun, key to french doors
           Alex: club tie (in pocket)

LIGHTING PLOT

Interior. A lounge. The same scene throughout. Practical fittings required: standard lamp, desk lamp.

ACT I Scene 1	Afternoon	
To open:	General interior lighting	
Cue 1	**Alex:** ". . . it certainly is . . ." *Lights fade to black-out*	(Page 15)

ACT I Scene 2	Evening	
To open:	Darkness	
Cue 2	When ready *Bring up general interior lighting*	(Page 15)
Cue 3	**Cathy:** ". . . I'm sure we'll be able to liven it up somehow." *Lights fade to black-out*	(Page 25)

ACT I Scene 3	Night	
To open:	Darkness	
Cue 4	When ready *Bring up soft interior lighting/lamplight*	(Page 25)
Cue 5	**Alex** goes to bottom of the staircase, turns off the lights, leaving the staircase and desk lights on *Bring general lighting down so only stair lighting and desk- lamp lighting remains*	(Page 28)
Cue 6	**Alex** switches on the standard lamp *Switch on lamp by the french windows*	(Page 29)
Cue 7	**Alex:** "Ahhhh!" *Flash of lightning*	(Page 35)
Cue 8	**Alex** switches off the standard lamp *Snap off lamp*	(Page 35)
Cue 9	**Alex** switches off the desk lamp *Snap off desk lamp*	(Page 35)
Cue 10	**Alex:** ". . . I don't suppose it has . . ." *Lightning*	(Page 35)

ACT II SCENE 1 Morning

To open: Bright sunny lighting

Cue 11   **Alex:** "Inspector—the very thought ..."   (page 50)
                    Lights fade to black-out

ACT II SCENE 2 Morning

To open: Bright sunny lighting

Cue 12   **Alex:** "Not—necessarily."   (page 58)
                    Lights fade to black-out

ACT II SCENE 3 Late evening

To open: General interior lighting including
                    lamplight

No cues

EFFECTS PLOT

ACT I

Cue 1   **Tony** opens the french windows   (Page 1)
Waves crashing against the cliffs

Cue 2   **Tony** leaves by the french windows   (Page 11)
Waves crashing

Cue 3   **Alex:** ''Damn that woman.''   (Page 16)
Taxi pulling up

Cue 4   **Dinah:** ''. . . the room feels so—oppressive.'' (Page 16)
Taxi pulling away

Cue 5   **Dinah:** ''. . . affair has other advantages.''   (Page 22)
Van pulling up

Cue 6   **Alex:** ''That's probably Cathy.''   (Page 22)
A grinding of gears

Cue 7   **Dinah** sits writing at desk   (Page 28)
The sound of the sea; curtains at french windows blow inward

Cue 8   **Dinah:** ''Why did he act so strangely?''   (Page 30)
Thunder

Cue 9   **Alex:** ''I don't understand you at all.''   (Page 32)
Roll of thunder

Cue 10 **Alex** goes to french windows   (Page 34)
Roll of thunder

Cue 11 **Alex:** ''. . . I don't suppose it has . . .''   (Page 35)
Thunder rolls

ACT II

Cue 12 As **Alex** enters through the french windows (Page 36)
Sea sounds

Cue 13 **Weaver:** ''. . . There's an exciting day for you.'' (Page 39)
Telephone rings

Cue 14 **Alex** stands in front of sofa, thinking   (Page 60)
The sound of the sea; curtains at french windows blow inward

Cue 15 **Dinah:** ''Alex . . . for God's sake—''   (Page 70)
Police siren

www.ingramcontent.com/pod-product-compliance
Lightning Source LLC
LaVergne TN
LVHW051759080426
835511LV00018B/3354